THE IMPORTANCE OF

Cleopatra

by
Don Nardo

Lucent Books, P.O. Box 289011, San Diego, CA 92198-9011

These and other titles are included in The Importance Of biography series:

Cleopatra	Margaret Mead
Christopher Columbus	Michelangelo
Marie Curie	Wolfgang Amadeus Mozart
Thomas Edison	Napoleon
Albert Einstein	Richard M. Nixon
Benjamin Franklin	Jackie Robinson
Galileo Galilei	Anwar Sadat
Thomas Jefferson	Margaret Sanger
Chief Joseph	Mark Twain
Malcolm X	H.G. Wells

Library of Congress Cataloging-in-Publication Data

Nardo, Don, 1947-
    Cleopatra / by Don Nardo
        p. cm.—(The Importance of)
    Includes bibliographical references and index.
Summary: Examines the life and reign of the woman who ruled Egypt from 51 to 30 B.C. and discusses her relationship with two powerful Roman leaders, Julius Caesar and Mark Antony.
    ISBN 1-56006-023-9 (acid-free paper)
    1. Cleopatra, Queen of Egypt. d. 30 B.C.—Juvenile literature. 2. Egypt—Quenns—Biography—Juvenile literature. [1. Cleopatra, Queen of Egypt, d. 30 B.C. 2. Kings, queens, rulers, etc.]
I.Title. II. Series.
DT92.7.N37   1994
932'.021'092—dc20   92-11079
[B]   CIP
                                                                  AC

Copyright 1994 by Lucent Books, Inc., P.O. Box 289011, San Diego, California, 92198-9011

Printed in the U.S.A.

Contents

Foreword

THE IMPORTANCE OF biography series deals with individuals who have made a unique contribution to history. The editors of the series have deliberately chosen to cast a wide net and include people from all fields of endeavor. Individuals from politics, music, art, literature, philosophy, science, sports, and religion are all represented. In addition, the editors did not restrict the series to individuals whose accomplishments have helped change the course of history. Of necessity, this criterion would have eliminated many whose contribution was great, though limited. Charles Darwin, for example, was responsible for radically altering the scientific view of the natural history of the world. His achievements continue to impact the study of science today. Others, such as Chief Joseph of the Nez Percé, played a pivotal role in the history of their own people. While Joseph's influence does not extend much beyond the Nez Percé, his nonviolent resistance to white expansion and his continuing role in protecting his tribe and his homeland remain an inspiration to all.

These biographies are more than factual chronicles. Each volume attempts to emphasize an individual's contributions both in his or her own time and for posterity. For example, the voyages of Christopher Columbus opened the way to European colonization of the New World. Unquestionably, his encounter with the New World brought monumental changes to both Europe and the Americas in his day. Today, however, the broader impact of Columbus's voyages is being critically scrutinized. *Christopher Columbus*, as well as every biography in The Importance Of series, includes and evaluates the most recent scholarship available on each subject.

Each author includes a wide variety of primary and secondary source quotations to document and substantiate his or her work. All quotes are footnoted to show readers exactly how and where biographers derive their information, as well as provide stepping stones to further research. These quotations enliven the text by giving readers eyewitness views of the life and times of each individual covered in The Importance Of series.

Finally, each volume is enhanced by photographs, bibliographies, chronologies, and comprehensive indexes. For both the casual reader and the student engaged in research, The Importance Of biographies will be a fascinating adventure into the lives of people who have helped shape humanity's past, present, and will continue to shape its future.

Important Dates in the Life of Cleopatra

B.C.

332 Alexander the Great liberates Egypt from Persian control.

323 Alexander dies and his generals fight over his empire.

305 Alexander's former general Ptolemy declares himself king of Egypt, establishing a Greek ruling dynasty.

Ptolemy XII, Auletes, Cleopatra's father, becomes king.

80

69 Cleopatra born

Caesar, Pompey, and Crassus form the First Triumvirate.

60 Auletes and Cleopatra travel to Rome to gain Roman support.

Auletes dies; Cleopatra becomes queen.

57 Cleopatra driven from Alexandria by her brother Ptolemy XIII.

51

49 Caesar assassinated in Roman Senate.

Caesar defeats Pompey at Pharsalus in Greece; Pompey slain in Egypt; Cleopatra regains Egyptian throne.

48

44 Antony and Octavian defeat Caesar's murderers at Philippi.

43 Antony, Octavian, and Lepidus form the Second Triumvirate.

42 Antony and Octavian sign Treaty of Brundisium; Antony leaves Cleopatra and marries Octavian's sister Octavia.

41 Antony and Cleopatra are lovers in Alexandria.

40

37 Antony and Cleopatra are reunited.

36 Antony's campaign against Parthia ends in failure.

34 Antony publicly proclaims Cleopatra "Queen of Kings."

33-32 Antony and Cleopatra prepare for war against Rome.

31 Octavian defeats Antony and Cleopatra at Actium in Greece.

30 Antony and Cleopatra commit suicide; Rome absorbs Egypt.

Fact Versus Fiction

Without doubt, Cleopatra VII, queen of Egypt from 51 to 30 B.C., is one of the most famous and controversial figures in history. Her fame rests primarily on her intimate relationships with Julius Caesar and Mark Antony, two of the most powerful men in the world in her day. Accounts

An ancient Roman statue of Cleopatra VII. Queen of Egypt from 51 to 30 B.C., she is renowned for her bold leadership and scandalous love affairs.

written about her when she was living describe her as bold, adventurous, ambitious, scheming, and sexually promiscuous. Because of these tales, which also describe her fabulously grand and extravagant life-style, she became a legend in her own time. Later stories emphasized how she had lived and died for love, and over the centuries her highly romantic legend continued to grow. Her deeds became the subject of numerous poems, plays, books, and motion pictures, and millions found her image as a colorful, powerful, and accomplished woman fascinating and compelling. The nineteenth-century French writer Théophile Gautier called her

> the most complete woman ever to have existed, the most womanly woman and the most queenly queen, a person to be wondered at, to whom the poets have been able to add nothing, and whom dreamers find always at the end of their dreams.[1]

Yet despite the large mass of material based on Cleopatra's life, very little factual, unbiased information about her exists. This is because most of the original stories about her were either penned by or based upon the writings of Roman authors, who disliked her and attempted to smear her name. According to these authors, she was greedy, dishonest, selfish, immoral, and a poor ruler. The Romans had three reasons for hating Cleopatra, the queen of Egypt. First, she was a foreigner, and the Romans looked down on and distrusted nearly all non-Romans. Second, she was a female ruler, and the Romans believed that women were, for the most part, unfit to rule men. According to the Greek historian Dio Cassius, the powerful Roman Octavian said of Cleopatra and of her Egyptian subjects:

> We Romans are the rulers of the greatest and best parts of the world, and yet we find ourselves spurned [rejected] and trampled upon by a woman of Egypt. This disgraces our fathers. . . . [Our ancestors] would be cut to the heart if ever they knew that we have been overcome by this pestilence [disease] of a woman. Would we not utterly dishonor ourselves if . . . [we] meekly endured the insults of this rabble, the natives of . . . Egypt? . . . They worship reptiles and beasts as gods . . . [and are] most backward in courage. Worst of all, they are not ruled by a man, but are the slaves of a woman.[2]

The third reason the Romans had for hating Cleopatra was their belief that she had manipulated and corrupted Caesar and Antony, two "noble and honorable" Romans. In Roman eyes, this was an evil and terrible deed.

Because this negative, partly fictional image created by the Roman propagandists was perpetuated through the ages, more positive evidence about Cleopatra and her achievements has been largely ignored. This evidence suggests that she was intelligent, resourceful, and an able ruler,

Elizabeth Taylor's portrayal of Cleopatra was one of the most memorable ever.

in many ways a role model for future generations of women. As writer Lucy Hughes-Hallet put it:

> In the years when she lived loverless in Egypt and devoted herself to the important . . . work of government, Cleopatra slips from sight. Just as a country will drop out of the news during periods of peace and prosperity, so Cleopatra, the able administrator with a scandal-free public life, was not good copy [popular news].[3]

It is perhaps one of the oddities of human nature that people throughout history have tended to perpetuate the lies about Cleopatra because these are often more interesting and sensational than the facts. Today it is often difficult, if not impossible, to separate the facts from the fiction. So she remains, and will remain for future ages, a supremely romantic, mysterious, and larger-than-life figure.

1 Egypt and Rome: The World of Cleopatra's Childhood

The seventh of Egypt's royal rulers bearing the name of Cleopatra was born in 69 B.C. Her father was Ptolemy XII, popularly called Auletes, or the Piper, because of his skill as a flute player. The identity of her mother remains unclear. But it is likely that Cleopatra's parents were Auletes and his own sister, Cleopatra Tryphaina. Such marriages between siblings were common in ancient royal families, particularly in Egypt.

At the time of Cleopatra's birth, Egypt, located in northeastern Africa along the southern shore of the Mediterranean Sea, was both a poor and a prosperous country. It was poor in the sense that most Egyptians were farmers and laborers living in extreme poverty. By contrast, the land they worked was rich and produced large quantities of grain and other foodstuffs. While this bounty kept the common people fed, the government and a few rich landowners claimed most surplus food and traded much of it to foreign countries. Egypt's rulers and wealthy nobility, who made up only a tiny fraction of the population, were also rich in gold and other precious metals and stones and enjoyed lavish life-styles.

But despite the prosperity of Egypt's upper crust, the country was politically unstable and militarily weak. A third-rate power in the Mediterranean, Egypt, like its neighbors, was dominated and intimi-

When Cleopatra was born, Egypt, a land known for its great monuments, had already been a center of world culture for millennia.

dated by Rome. In the mid-first century B.C., Rome was the most powerful nation on earth, commanding an empire that included Italy, Spain, central Europe, northern Africa, Greece, and Asia Minor, what is now Turkey. Egypt still remained independent, but dared not challenge Roman might. As historian Naphtali Lewis put it, "The entire Mediterranean Sea was a Roman lake and those who lived on and around it looked to Rome as the arbiter [controller] of their fortunes."[4]

Land of the Pharaohs

But the Mediterranean balance of power had not always been tipped against Egypt. Many centuries before, the country had been one of the cradles of human culture and the most powerful and prosperous land in the Mediterranean world. As far back as 6000 B.C., and perhaps even earlier, when most Europeans were Stone Age hunters, people were farming the rich soil lying along the banks of Egypt's Nile River. Stretching some 4,180 miles, this longest of the world's rivers flows from the mountains of east-central Africa northward into what became known as Upper Egypt, then farther north through Lower Egypt, to empty into the Mediterranean. Historian Lionel Casson explains:

The Valley of the Nile was in truth a cradle of civilization, a place which assured the society that arose there an infancy snug and secure, unaffected by what went on in the regions round about. On three sides deserts formed a barrier, and on the fourth, the sea. . . . The river, when properly handled,

guaranteed the richest crops in the ancient world. In Upper Egypt the sun shone all day all year, while Lower Egypt received hardly more than a touch of rain; the Egyptians were blessedly ignorant of . . . violent weather. . . . They conceived of the world as stable and benign, and it is easy to see why, in their isolation and security, they did so. . . . Since there was no rain, all water had to come from the river. Every year it flooded on schedule and provided plenty—so long as people worked together to build the dikes, canals, catch basins, and other devices needed to conserve it and were reasonable about sharing it.[5]

The cities of ancient Egypt hugged the banks of the life-giving Nile River.

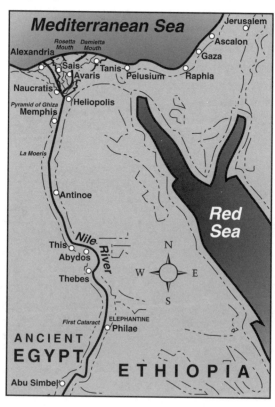

The pharaohs of ancient Egypt were believed to be gods. This ancient coronation ceremony takes place amid mystic rituals as well as royal splendor.

sive chapter in the history of art and architecture was begun. The temple of Karnak [in the city of Thebes] contains the greatest colonnaded [column-lined] hall ever erected by man. . . . Such temples . . . at Thebes were seen through the deep green of clustering palms, among towering obelisks [stone monuments], and colossal statues of the Pharaohs. The whole was bright with color, and flashing at many a point with bands of sheet gold and silver. Mirrored in the unruffled surface of the temple lake, it made a picture of such splendor as the ancient world had never seen before.[6]

Later pharaohs continued to expand Egyptian power and splendor, erecting new cities along the Nile. Some built the giant pyramids at Gizeh in Lower Egypt as

These magnificent ruins of the temple of Karnak in Thebes only hint at Egypt's former glory.

By about 3000 B.C. Egypt had grown into a prosperous and powerful nation ruled by kings known as pharaohs. Absolute monarchs whose word was law, they were looked upon as living gods. The early pharaohs raised armies and invaded Nubia, the African land located south of Egypt, as well as Palestine in the Middle East, the Asian region bordering Egypt in the northeast. These successful conquests made Egypt the strongest and richest land in the world at the time. According to historian James Henry Breasted:

The wealth which these Egyptian emperors captured in Asia and Nubia brought them power and magnificence unknown to the world before, especially as shown in their vast and splendid buildings. A new and impres-

The mysterious Sphinx and the Great Pyramid of Gizeh are perhaps the two most famous Egyptian monuments. Even today, many people believe these structures hold undiscovered secrets and magical powers.

their own burial monuments. For nearly two thousand years Egypt remained a nation to be both feared and envied.

Under Foreign Rule

Eventually, however, Egypt's power declined, largely because it was attacked by nations with stronger, better-equipped armies. Whereas Egyptian soldiers fought with weapons made from copper and bronze, new empires that rose in Asia Minor and the Middle East had learned to use iron, a much stronger metal. Egypt, which had no natural sources of iron, was at a clear disadvantage. Beginning in the twelfth century B.C., foreign invaders re-

peatedly usurped the Egyptian throne. In the seventh century B.C., the warlike Assyrians, from the region that is now Iraq, overran Egypt. And in the sixth century B.C., the mighty Persian Empire, centered in what is now Iran, eclipsed Assyria's domain, including Egypt. Like the Assyrians, the Persians oppressed the Egyptians, denying them the right to rule themselves and taxing them heavily.

The Egyptians were thrilled, therefore, when the Greek armies of Alexander the Great defeated the Persians in the 330s B.C. When Alexander entered Egypt in triumph in 332 B.C., the people welcomed him as a liberator. But Egypt was not free. It had merely become part of Alexander's own Greek empire, one that eventually stretched from eastern Europe to India.

Nevertheless, the Egyptians at first found Greek rule enlightened and fair. The Greeks respected Egyptian ways and beliefs, offering little interference with local customs. And Alexander founded a magnificent new city along the Mediterranean coast (calling it Alexandria after himself). This port quickly became the busiest and most prosperous in the ancient world.

In 323 B.C., less than ten years after marching into Egypt, Alexander died suddenly at the age of thirty-three. Almost immediately, his generals began fighting for possession of his mighty empire. After a bloody power struggle that lasted for several decades, three of these generals, Anti-

(Above) After Alexander's death, Ptolemy, one of Alexander's generals, received Egypt as his portion of Alexander's empire. Cleopatra was descended from Ptolemy.

(Below) The youthful Alexander surveys his army's siege of one of the numerous lands that fell under his conquest. His empire included Egypt, where he built the magnificent city of Alexandria.

gonus, Seleucus, and Ptolemy, emerged victorious and divided Alexander's empire into three Greek kingdoms. Because the Greeks called themselves Hellenes, these political divisions became known as the Hellenistic kingdoms. In the early third century B.C. Ptolemy established the Ptolemaic kingdom, which consisted mainly of Egypt, and founded a new dynasty, or ruling family, the royal line that would later produce the legendary Cleopatra.

Ptolemaic Egypt

The Ptolemies ran Egypt as it had always been run, as an absolute monarchy. For the average Egyptian, apart from the fact that the royal family was now Greek, nothing had really changed. The Ptolemaic

A Remarkable and Fascinating Place

Under the Ptolemies, Alexandria was perhaps the most important commercial and cultural center in the Mediterranean. In their book Cleopatra, *Dorothy and Thomas Hoobler set the scene.*

"At their capital of Alexandria, the Ptolemies were active patrons of . . . culture. Ptolemy I had established a library and museum [university] where scholars from all over the Mediterranean world came to study. By Cleopatra's time, the library contained over 700,000 volumes. Much of what remains of the great literature, philosophy, and science of Greece came to the modern world through Alexandria. It was in Alexandria that Eratosthenes became the first man to measure the circumference of the earth, and the scientist Aristarchus formulated the theory that the earth revolves around the sun. It was here that Euclid systematized geometry and wrote his *Elements of Geometry.* His ideas form the basis of what is taught today in high school. (The first Ptolemy asked Euclid if geometry could be made easier to learn. Euclid's famous answer was "There is no royal road [to learning].") Cleopatra spent most of her life in Alexandria. A remarkable and fascinating place, it was the scene of many of her greatest triumphs, and of her ultimate defeat. Alexander the Great had picked this site for his capital because of its magnificent harbor. In the middle of the harbor was Pharos Island, at the tip of which was one of the Wonders of the Ancient World—a lighthouse whose fire, magnified by mirrors, could be seen 35 miles out to sea. A mole, or causeway, connected the island and the mainland, dividing the harbor into two sections. To the east was the Great Harbor; to the west, the Safe Return Harbor. A series of canals connected the harbor to the Nile River."

An artist's conception of how ancient Alexandria must have appeared. Its glory rivaled Rome's.

kings and queens, like many pharaohs before them, both Egyptian and foreign, were largely mediocre and unsympathetic rulers who cared little for the sufferings of the masses. Most people had little or nothing to look forward to in life: they continued to toil in the fields, on building projects, or in the state-owned mines. Workers in the Ptolemaic mines labored under particularly harsh conditions. The Greek geographer Agatharchides described work in an Egyptian gold mine during the second century B.C.:

> Those who are young and strong quarry the gleaming stone with iron picks, delivering their blows not with any particular skill but just force. They cut numerous galleries [tunnels] in the rock. . . . They do their quarrying with [oil] lamps bound to their foreheads. . . . [The foreman] never fails to administer punishment with the whip. Young boys, creeping through the galleries . . . laboriously collect what has fallen down on the gallery floor and carry it outside. . . . [T]he men who are still under thirty . . . are given stone mortars, and they pound the rock vigorously . . . until they have made the biggest piece the size of a pea. . . . Now starts the work of the women who . . . take their places, three to a turning bar, and grind away. They are a sad sight. . . . All who suffer the fate just described feel that death is more desirable than life.[7]

The harshness of their rule was not the only thing that made most of the Ptolemies unpopular with the Egyptians. Members of the royal line also refused to recognize traditional Egyptian gods and to learn the Egyptian language. This show of disrespect for the people created a cultural barrier between the Egyptians, whose worship and language remained unchanged, and the royal court, where Greek ways were supreme. Occasional nationalistic, or patriotic, rebellions occurred during the more than two centuries of Ptolemaic rule. But because of their wealth and complete control of the military, the kings easily quelled these disturbances.

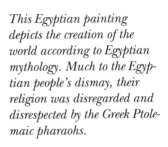

This Egyptian painting depicts the creation of the world according to Egyptian mythology. Much to the Egyptian people's dismay, their religion was disregarded and disrespected by the Greek Ptolemaic pharaohs.

The Circle of Popillius

The most famous demonstration of Roman force over a Hellenistic kingdom occurred in 167 B.C. According to the Greek historian Polybius in his Histories, *the Romans sent an ambassador named Popillius, who ordered Antiochus* "to end his war against Ptolemy at once and withdraw his army into Syria [in Palestine] within a stated time. The King read it and said he wanted to consult his friends about the new development. Whereupon Popillius did something [sudden and unexpected] and exceedingly arrogant, to all appearances. He was carrying a stick cut from a vine. With it he drew a circle around Antiochus and bade him give his reply to the communication right [away while still] in that circle. The king was taken aback [insulted] at this high-handed action, but after hesitating a little he said he would do everything required of him by the Romans."

While they commanded ultimate power in Egypt, however, the Ptolemies held little sway beyond Egyptian borders. They frequently fought with the rulers of the Hellenistic Seleucid kingdom, which included Palestine and most of the Middle East. The Ptolemies also came into contact with the Romans, whose military might was moving into the eastern Mediterranean during the third century B.C. The Romans, a practical people, recognized the potential of Egypt's vast grain supply for feeding Roman troops. So at first, Rome cultivated good relations with Egypt and offered to protect it from its enemies. In time, however, the Egyptian rulers became thoroughly intimidated by Roman power. Naphtali Lewis writes:

As Roman power spread eastward in the second century B.C., it came into conflict with one Hellenistic kingdom then another; but Egypt, Rome's friend of long standing, was not only left on the sidelines of those hostilities, but was given protection by Rome on occasions when the need arose. Protection evolved . . . into protectorate [a country controlled by a superior power]. Long before the last Cleopatra ascended the throne of her ancestors, Egypt, though . . . still independent, had become in reality a client [dependent] state of all-powerful Rome.[8]

Life in the Alexandrian Court

It was this weakened Egypt, a pale shadow of the powerful pharaonic empire of millennia past, that Auletes inherited when he became King Ptolemy XII in 80 B.C. Like the leaders who had immediately preceded him, he recognized that Egypt, though rich in gold and grain, was a third-rate power. As his father and grandfather had, he feared that Rome might at any moment flex its military muscle, annex Egypt, and make it a Roman province. So Auletes carried on the Ptolemaic policy of appeasing Rome and its whims.

For a number of years, this policy paid off for Auletes and his court. The royal family and high Egyptian officials enjoyed a life of excitement and unbounded luxury in Alexandria, still a thriving center of trade and commerce. The city, rivaled in splendor only by Rome, boasted many impressive palaces, government buildings, and other important structures. According to the Greek geographer Strabo:

The shape of the city's area is like a *chlamys* [a Greek tunic]. The two long

During the Ptolemaic dynasty, Alexandria, its capital, became the world's center of learning. This drawing depicts a chamber within its famous library.

sides are those washed by the [Mediterranean] . . . with a diameter of some 30 *stadia* [one *stadium* equals about 606 feet], while the short sides are the isthmuses [narrow land strips], each 7 or 8 *stadia* wide. . . . The place as a whole is intersected by streets practicable for horse-riding and chariot-driving, and by two that are very broad, extending to more than [100 feet] in breadth. . . . And the city contains most beautiful public precincts as well as the royal palaces, which make up a fourth or even a third of the whole circuit. As each of the kings out of a love of splendor used to add some fresh adornment to the monuments, so also he [constructed his own new] residence besides those already built. Thus, to cite the poet [the Greek Homer], "There is building on [top of] building."[9]

The royal family grew over the years. In the 70s B.C., Auletes and his queen had two daughters—Berenice and Cleopatra Tryphaina, named after her mother. The queen died in 69 B.C., the same year Cleopatra VII was born. Afterward, Auletes had another daughter, Arsinoe, and two boys, called Ptolemy XIII and Ptolemy XIV, whose mother or mothers remain unknown.

These siblings grew up amidst the lavish trappings of the Egyptian court. They ate the best foods, wore beautiful clothes made of the finest materials, witnessed elaborate court ceremonies and entertainments, and had as many expensive toys and pets as they desired. They also had personal tutors and servants, as well as the protection and obedience of the many different kinds of people who lived and

This scene from a 1934 film version of Cleopatra's life depicts Cleopatra's grand lifestyle.

worked within the palace grounds. Lionel Casson explains:

> In ancient Egypt's way of life, the various social strata did not live apart in distincitive areas but were intermingled within households or institutional complexes. Within the bounds of the palace there dwelt together the [king], his queen, children, and the rest of the royal family; the officials of state whose duties required their close presence; many of the scribes [clerks] employed in the central administration; the royal physicians; the royal guards; the valets, maids, and all others involved in the housekeeping; the bakers, brewers, butchers, cooks . . . all others concerned with feeding the multitude that ate at the palace tables; the weavers and tailors who made the royal wardrobe; the sculptors who carved the royal portraits . . . the drivers of the royal chariots . . . crews of the royal yachts, and so on.[10]

In general, Cleopatra and her siblings en-joyed comfortable, carefree, and sheltered lives, protected from the grim realities of the poverty and toils of the common people.

Events Grim and Sordid

But Auletes could not shelter his family from the knowledge that most Egyptians still resented the Ptolemies. Auletes himself was particularly unpopular because he regularly mismanaged government money and thereby caused economic conditions in the country to worsen. One of his worst mistakes was to debase the coinage by reducing the proportion of silver in coins to one-third. This made money worth less, and the cost of living rose sharply. At the same time, Auletes tried to make up for his financial blunders by imposing heavy and unfair new taxes. All these hardships caused increased unrest among the people, and the king feared open rebellion.

In 59 B.C., Auletes attempted to

The Death of a Cat

Though Greek, Cleopatra grew up in and was influenced by a highly religious Egyptian society that regarded some animals as special and sacred. One of the most sacred was the cat. In his work Library of History, *the Roman historian Diodorus described a violent response to a cat's death.*

"So deeply implanted in the hearts of their common folk is a superstitious regard for these animals and so ineradicable [deep-rooted] are the emotions each cherishes as to their due honor, that once, at a time when Ptolemy [XII, Auletes] their King had not yet been given the appellation [title] of Friend [of Rome] and the people were courting with all possible zeal the favor of the Embassy from Italy [Roman ambassador] when visiting Egypt, and in their fear [of Rome] were preoccupied with giving no pretext for complaint or war—yet when one of the Romans killed a cat and the mob rushed in a crowd to his house, neither the officials sent by the King to beg the man off, nor the fear of Rome felt by all the people, was enough to save him from punishment, even though the act had been an accident. And this incident I relate, not from hearsay, but having seen it with my own eyes during the visit I made to Egypt."

An ancient Egyptian statue of a sacred cat.

Pompey (left) and Julius Caesar (right), along with another Roman general, Crassus, ruled the Roman Republic during Cleopatra's time. Cleopatra's father bought Caesar and Pompey's support for his reign, but they charged him a huge sum to simply acknowledge him as king of Egypt.

strengthen his position, both at home and abroad, by making a deal with the Romans. He approached two powerful Roman generals—Julius Caesar and Pompey. At the time, they, along with another important Roman named Crassus, held power in Rome through an unofficial alliance later referred to as the First Triumvirate, or rule of three. Auletes asked Caesar and Pompey to recognize him publicly as the rightful ruler of Egypt, something no Roman leader had done yet, and to declare him a "friend and ally" of Rome. Auletes hoped such lofty titles would make him more feared in Egypt. Caesar and Pompey agreed but demanded that the king pay 6,000 talents, a huge sum of money, to seal the bargain. Because he lacked the funds, Auletes borrowed the money from a wealthy Roman.

But Auletes' plan failed and his trou-bles worsened. In the following two years he uncovered several plots against himself and the government. In 57 B.C., he traveled to Rome to try to get more Roman support, and some ancient sources suggest that Cleopatra, then twelve, may have gone with him. In their absence, the king's daughter Cleopatra Tryphaina seized his throne. Auletes was desperate. He promised a prominent Roman named Aulus Gabinius 10,000 talents if he would lead Roman troops to Alexandria and recapture the Egyptian throne. The events that followed were grim and sordid. While Gabinius and Auletes were on the way to Egypt, a group of the king's supporters killed Cleopatra Tryphaina, and her sister Berenice grabbed power for herself. This was a fatal mistake. Gabinius easily restored Auletes to power, and the king's first official act was to execute Berenice.

This classical engraving depicting Cleopatra shows her robed in Egyptian attire but with classical Roman face and hairstyle.

For all his troubles in regaining power, however, Auletes' new reign was a short one. He died in the spring of 51 B.C. According to his will, Cleopatra, now aged eighteen, and her ten-year-old brother Ptolemy XIII, were to rule jointly.

An Awesome Challenge

To Roman leaders and rulers in other countries as well, the young girl who had inherited the Egyptian throne was an un-known quantity. To some degree she still is, because no precise descriptions of her have survived. Writing much later, the ancient writer Plutarch declared that "Her actual beauty . . . was not in itself so remarkable that none could be compared with her, or that no one could see her without being struck by it."[11] Indeed, surviving coins bearing her image depict her as having a large hooked nose and a jutting chin. This is in marked contrast to her image as a ravishing beauty in later stories, paintings, and films. But what she may have lacked in good looks, Cleopatra

Two Strikes Against Her

On becoming queen of Egypt, Cleopatra had to face dealing with the powerful Romans. In her book Cleopatra: Histories, Dreams and Distortions, *writer Lucy Hallet explains that in Roman eyes Cleopatra immediately had two strikes against her. She was a foreigner and a woman. This prejudice has been handed down through the ages.*

"Cleopatra was Rome's enemy, and we in the West are Rome's heirs. The notion of Cleopatra that we have inherited identifies her primarily as being the adversary, the Other. Her otherness is twofold. She is an Oriental [person from an eastern or Asian rather than a western or European society], and she is a woman. Even in her lifetime her legend was already shaped by the two overlapping chauvinisms [prejudices] of race and sex, for in a man's world every woman is a foreigner. According to the legend, Cleopatra and the people of her court are dishonest, self-indulgent, sex-fixated and . . . feminine. . . . Her Roman adversaries embody the "masculine" virtues of patriotism, discipline, sexual abstemiousness [moderation], and readiness for war. From Rome we have inherited not only this language of racial and sexual stereotyping (which has remained extraordinarily constant for over two thousand years) but also the habits of mind which decree not only that the "Roman" qualities are peculiarly masculine, but also that they are virtues."

apparently made up in charm and personality. According to Plutarch:

> The contact of her presence, if you lived with her, was irresistible; the attraction of her person, joining with the charm of her conversation, and the character that attended all she said or did, was something bewitching. It was a pleasure merely to hear the sound of her voice.[12]

It was fortunate for Cleopatra that she possessed such strong character and social skills because she sorely needed every strength and asset she could muster. The sheltered life of her childhood had come to an abrupt end. She now faced the dangerous prospect of ruling a people who resented her and the awesome challenge of surviving in a world controlled by arrogant and power-hungry men.

2 Caesar and Cleopatra: The Quest for Power

It was a troubled throne that Cleopatra ascended in the spring of 51 B.C. Almost immediately, serious tensions and rivalries erupted between her and her youthful brother Ptolemy XIII. The boy's regent, or adult adviser and protector, was the eunuch Pothinus, the most powerful figure in the Egyptian court. Resenting Cleopatra and wanting to see Ptolemy become sole ruler of Egypt, Pothinus took advantage of every opportunity to discredit the new queen. Cleopatra also had to deal with serious domestic problems for which there were no easy solutions. In the first two years of her reign the Nile did not rise high enough to irrigate all the fields, and this resulted in food shortages. The crisis intensified when many farmers and labor-

The shoreline of Alexandria, capital of Ptolemaic Egypt. The tall obelisk in the foreground is known as Cleopatra's needle.

ers went into hiding to avoid paying their taxes. Thanks to Pothinus, who unfairly blamed her for these and other pressing problems, Cleopatra became increasingly unpopular in the Egyptian court. Finally, in September 49 B.C., she was forced to flee from Alexandria into hiding in the desert.

But Cleopatra's exile from her own court was short-lived. Fortunately for her, major political upheavals were then occurring in Rome. The triumvirate had been shattered. First Crassus had been killed in an unsuccessful war against the Parthians,

Caesar leads his army across the Rubicon River into Rome in 49 B.C., defying the Senate's orders. The ensuing civil war divided Rome but brought Caesar and Cleopatra together.

a Middle Eastern people who were threatening Rome's eastern provinces. Then a bloody civil war had broken out between Caesar and Pompey. Cleopatra reasoned that one or both of these men would seek Egyptian grain and money to support his troops. She also realized that sooner or later one of them would win the war and that Egypt would have to deal with him. Unlike Ptolemy, Pothinus, and Cleopatra's other adversaries in the court, who hated and resisted Roman influence, Cleopatra recognized the political reality of the day. Rome controlled the Mediterranean world. Those who resisted the Romans would suffer, while those who cooperated with them would benefit. So she boldly enlisted Roman aid in regaining her throne. Showing unusual courage, resourcefulness, and political skill for one so young, she not only achieved this goal, but also won the support and love of the most powerful man in the world.

A Deadly Trap

In 48 B.C., after Cleopatra had spent many months in exile, the power struggle between Caesar and Pompey reached its climax. Caesar decisively defeated his opponent in a major battle at Pharsalus in central Greece. Though humiliated, Pompey refused to give up the struggle and turned to Egyptian leaders for protection and support. Apparently, he intended to use Egyptian money to help raise another army and carry on the war. In his *War Commentaries*, Caesar recorded:

> It happened that the boy-king Ptolemy was at Pelusium [in northern Egypt]

Caesar's Alexandrian Notes

The Civil Wars, *Julius Caesar's first-person account of some of his own exploits, briefly describes the arrival in Egypt of the Roman leader. In a chapter titled "Operations in Egypt," Caesar tells about the young king, Ptolemy XIII, and the Egyptian political situation at the time.*

"Because of the king's youth, his tutor, a eunuch called Pothinus, was in real control of the kingdom. He began by expressing among his own party [followers] his grief and indignation at the idea of the king's being called upon to come [to Caesar] and plead his cause. Then, finding accomplices among the king's friends, he [Pothinus] secretly withdrew the army from Pelusium and brought it to Alexandria, where he gave supreme command of all forces to the Achillas whom we have already mentioned. Achillas was promised rewards in the name both of Pothinus and the king, and was told by messenger or by letter what Pothinus wanted him to do. Now in the will of the late King Ptolemy [XII, Auletes], the heirs were the elder of the two sons [Ptolemy XIII] and the elder of the two daughters [Cleopatra]. In the same will Ptolemy called upon the Roman people, in the name of all the gods and in conformance with [obeying] the treaty he had made at Rome, to see that his last wishes were carried ut. One copy of the will had been taken by his ambassadors to Rome to be placed in the treasury, but political disturbances had prevented its being officially deposited there and so it had been left in the keeping of Pompey. A duplicate copy was left under seal at Alexandria."

with a large army. He was at [odds] with his sister Cleopatra, whom he had driven from the throne a few months earlier by the help of his relatives and friends. . . . Pompey sent [messengers] to Ptolemy asking him, in view of the close bonds of friendship and hospitality that there had been between himself and his father [Auletes], to receive him into Alexandria and to use his power to protect him in his misfortune. After making this formal request, Pompey's messengers began to speak more freely with the Egyptian king's soldiers, urging them to do their duty to Pompey and not to regard his cause as lost. Among them were a number of Pompey's old soldiers whom Gabinius had taken over from his army in Syria and, at the end of his campaign, had left with Ptolemy Auletes, the father of the young king.[13]

Ptolemy, Pothinus, and Achillas, commander of Ptolemy's royal bodyguards, considered the situation. They decided that it would not be wise to back Pompey against Caesar. "It may be," Caesar later wrote, "that they were really afraid that Pompey might tamper with the loyalty of the royal army and occupy Alexandria and Egypt; or it may be that they regarded his prospects as hopeless and acted according to the common rule by which a man's friends become his enemies in adversity."[14] Whatever their motivation, Ptolemy and his advisers laid a trap for Pompey. When the general and his wife Cornelia arrived off the Egyptian coast, they were surprised that no royal welcoming party awaited them. Instead, Achillas and Sempronius, a Roman soldier in Ptolemy's pay, rowed out in a small boat and greeted Pompey. The Roman historian Appian described the springing of the trap:

Pompey's suspicions were aroused by . . . the fact that the king himself

(Above) Pompey flees Pharsalus after his defeat by Caesar. He later appealed to Cleopatra's brother Ptolemy for aid but was assassinated (right) by former Roman soldiers as they rowed him from his galley to the Alexandrian court.

did not come to meet him. . . . Nevertheless, he entered the skiff [boat]. . . . While rowing to the shore all were silent, and this made him still more suspicious. Finally . . . recognizing Sempronius as a Roman soldier . . . he turned to him and said, "Do I not know you, comrade?" The other nodded and, as Pompey turned away, he immediately gave him the first stab and the others followed his example. Pompey's wife and friends who saw this at a distance cried out, lifting their hands to heaven. . . . Then they sailed away in all haste as from an enemy's country.[15]

Achillas and his men cut off Pompey's head and delivered it to Ptolemy and Pothinus. The king and his regent hoped the grisly trophy would please Caesar who, according to rumors, was headed for Egypt in pursuit of his adversary. They expected Caesar to thank them and then depart, leaving them in charge of Egypt. Meanwhile, Cleopatra's spies kept her informed of what was happening as she waited for the right opportunity to act.

Caesar Captivated

Sure enough, Caesar arrived four days later with a small contingent of soldiers. Contrary to the expectations of Ptolemy and Pothinus, however, Caesar was far from pleased at seeing Pompey's severed head. Instead, he was outraged that a great Roman general had been so brutally murdered. He also showed no intention of leaving, as the Egyptian leaders had hoped. Caesar needed money to pay for

his campaigns and planned to get it from the Egyptian treasury. He claimed that Auletes' debts to wealthy Romans had not been paid in full and said that he, Caesar, was there to collect them.

But Caesar's demands had to wait while he was forced to deal with an unexpected situation. When his troops landed in Alexandria, the local soldiers and inhabitants thought that the Romans were attempting to seize the city and overthrow

Julius Caesar, Rome's most powerful figure, became romantically involved with Cleopatra and helped her regain Egypt's throne.

Battle for Alexandria

While Caesar and Cleopatra were trapped in the palace at Alexandria, Ptolemy's regent Pothinus ordered military leader Achillas to attack Caesar's small forces. In his War Commentaries, *Caesar recalled some of the fighting.*

"Achillas had an army which in numbers, quality, and military experience was very far from being contemptible [bad]. There were twenty thousand men under arms. . . . Their numbers were augmented [increased] by men gathered together from the bands of pirates and robbers from Syria. . . . Confident in these troops of his and contemptuous [scornful] of the small numbers of my own army, Achillas seized Alexandria, except for that part of the town which we already held. In his first attack he tried to break into the palace where I was in residence, but was beaten off by the cohorts [bands of soldiers] which I had posted in the streets. At the same time fighting broke out in the harbor area. Here the struggle was the hardest of all. Street fighting was going on between scattered bodies of troops in different streets, and simultaneously large numbers of the enemy were trying to get possession of our warships. . . . The enemy realized that if they could gain possession of these ships, I should be left without a fleet, and they, with the harbor and the whole sea in their control, would be able to cut me off from both reinforcements and supplies. Consequently the fighting was of a most bitter character, as it was bound to be, for the enemy saw in this action the chance of a quick victory while we knew that our very existence depended on the result. In the end the success was ours."

the government. Caesar later recalled:

As soon as I landed I was greeted by the angry shouting of the soldiers whom the king had left to garrison [protect] the city, and I saw a great mob rushing toward me. This was because the *fasces* [symbols of Roman power] were being carried in front of me, and the whole crowd considered this to be an infringement of the royal authority. The disturbance was put down, but for several days on end rioting broke out as a result of mass demonstrations [against the Romans] and many of my soldiers were killed in all parts of the city.[16]

At this point, because he had not brought enough troops to deal with a full-scale uprising, Caesar might have wanted to take the money and leave. But strong seasonal prevailing winds kept his ships bottled up in the city's harbor. So he settled down in the royal palace to wait until the situation quieted.

Seeing her chance to appeal to Caesar, Cleopatra acted. According to Plutarch in his *Life of Caesar:*

> She took a small boat, and one only of her confidants [trusted followers], Apollodorus, the Sicilian, along with her, and in the dusk of the evening landed near the palace. She was at a loss how to get in undiscovered, till she thought of putting herself into the coverlet of a bed and lying at length, whilst Apollodorus tied up the bedding and carried it on his back through the gates to Caesar's apartment.[17]

Exactly what was said when Cleopatra climbed out of the bedding and confronted Caesar remains unknown. What is certain is that Caesar found her bold and captivating. And to the dismay of her brother and Pothinus, she and the most powerful Roman quickly became lovers. At the time she was twenty-one and he fifty-two.

Caesar proceeded to back Cleopatra in the royal power struggle, demanding that she and Ptolemy marry and rule jointly as Auletes had decreed in his will. Intimidated by Caesar, Ptolemy and Pothinus agreed to these demands. But they did not intend to keep their word. Near the end of 48 B.C. Pothinus ordered Achillas to take charge of the Egyptian army and surround the palace. Caesar and Cleopatra, along with a small force of Romans, were trapped. But ironically, so were Ptolemy and Pothinus, and the opposing parties coexisted in the palace for two months.

Finally, a series of violent events brought an end to this bizarre impasse. Cleopatra's sister Arsinoe, perhaps with Pothinus's blessing, slipped out of the palace, joined Achillas, and proclaimed herself ruler of Egypt. Hearing rumors that Pothinus was involved in this affair, Caesar had the eunuch executed. Ptolemy fled to join Achillas. Shortly afterward, Roman reinforcements arrived and Caesar easily defeated the Egyptian army at Lake Mareotis, a few miles from Alexandria. After the battle, Ptolemy's lifeless body, clad in golden armor, was found in the Nile. With Caesar's help, Cleopatra had man-

A nineteenth-century engraving depicts Caesar's surprise as Cleopatra emerges from her hiding place in his bedclothes. Her boldness immediately impressed him.

A Moonlit Encounter

Of the many literary and screen versions of the meeting between Caesar and the Egyptian queen, that depicted by playwright George Bernard Shaw in Caesar and Cleopatra *is one of the greatest. Shaw dispensed with Plutarch's description of the bedroll ruse and placed the meeting on a moonlit night at an Egyptian sphinx. In this excerpt from the scene, Cleopatra, shown as a frightened girl hiding from the Romans, does not realize the visitor is the mighty Caesar.*

"CAESAR O Sphinx. . . . My way hither was the way of destiny; for I am he of whose genius you are the symbol.

THE GIRL Old gentleman. . . .

CAESAR [surprised] Sphinx: you presume on your centuries. I am younger than you, but your voice is but a girl's voice as yet.

THE GIRL Climb up here quickly; or the Romans will come and eat you.

CAESAR [seeing her] A child at its breast! a divine child! . . . Who are you?

THE GIRL Cleopatra, queen of Egypt.

CAESAR Queen of the Gypsies, you mean.

CLEOPATRA You must not be disrespectful to me, or the Sphinx will let the Romans eat you.

CAESAR What a dream! What a magnificent dream! . . . What are you doing here at this time of night? Do you live here?

CLEOPATRA Of course not: I am the Queen; and I shall live in the palace at Alexandria when I have killed my brother, who drove me out of it. . . . Tell me: do you think the Romans have any sorcerers who could take us away from the Sphinx by magic?

CAESAR Why? Are you afraid of the Romans?

CLEOPATRA Oh, they would eat us if they caught us. They are barbarians. Their chief is called Julius Caesar. His father was a tiger and his mother a burning mountain. . . . They all have long noses, and ivory tusks, and little tails, and seven arms with a hundred arrows in each; and they live on human flesh.

CAESAR Would you like me to show you a real Roman?

CLEOPATRA [terrified] No. . . . I'm afraid—afraid of the Romans.

CAESAR Cleopatra: can you see my face well?

CLEOPATRA Yes. It is so white in the moonlight.

CAESAR Are you sure it is the moonlight that makes me look whiter than an Egyptian? Do you notice that I have a rather long nose?

CLEOPATRA Oh!

CAESAR It is a Roman nose, Cleopatra."

aged to overcome her opponents and regain her throne. Her personal quest for power had been successful.

Journeys in Egypt and Rome

Caesar, a practical man, realized that Cleopatra, as his lover and confidant, would make him and Rome a valuable ally. So he reinstalled her on the Egyptian throne with great pomp and ceremony. He also tried to please the Egyptians by having her, according to custom, marry her surviving brother, twelve-year-old Ptolemy XIV. Since this young Ptolemy had no powerful regent like Pothinus, Cleopatra was, in effect, sole ruler of the country.

Before leaving Egypt for Rome, Caesar

The temple at Luxor near Thebes was probably one of the sights enjoyed by Caesar and Cleopatra on their Nile cruise.

stayed a few months in order to enjoy Cleopatra's company and see some of the world-famous sights of Egypt. Caesar found the young queen to be intelligent, surprisingly well-read, fluent in several languages, and interested in learning all subjects. Together, the two slowly sailed up the great river running the length of the country. Appian wrote that Caesar, "ascended the Nile with 400 ships, exploring the country in company with Cleopatra and generally enjoying himself with her."[18] The number of ships suggested by Appian is probably an exaggeration, but there is no doubt that the two enjoyed the traditional opulent luxuries of Egyptian monarchs. Describing the magnificent setting of one of Caesar and Cleopatra's feasts, the Roman poet Lucan wrote:

> Great was the bustle as Cleopatra displayed
> a magnificence not yet adopted in Roman ways.
> A temple-size hall, too costly for an age
> corrupted with pleasure-spending. The ceiling panels
> blazed wealth, the rafters hidden in thick gold.
> Marble the walls shone. . . . The porch was ivory;
> Indian tortoise-shell, hand-colored, stood,
> inlaying doors, with emeralds in its spots. . . .
> A swarm of attendants [slaves and servants] too, a ministering mob,
> differing in age and race. On some was seen
> African hair, on others hair so fair
> Caesar declared the Rhineland [Germany] lacked such reds.[19]

The love affair between Caesar and Cleopatra came to life in this movie portrayal by Elizabeth Taylor and Rex Harrison.

Eventually, Caesar had to give up this lavish holiday to return to pressing duties in Rome. When he departed Egypt in 47 B.C., Cleopatra was carrying his child.

Cleopatra in Rome

About a year later, after taking part in some foreign military campaigns, Caesar finally celebrated his victory in what had become known in Rome as the Alexandrian War. He must have felt it fitting to have Cleopatra witness the festivities. The Roman historian Suetonius recorded that "he called her to Rome and did not let her leave until he had laden her with high honors and rich gifts, and allowed her to give his name to the child which she bore." Cleopatra named the boy Caesar-

ion. "In fact," Suetonius added, "according to certain Greek writers, this child was very like Caesar in looks and carriage."[20]

Cleopatra and her child likely attended Caesar's triumph, or victory parade, in which he prominently featured the former princess Arsinoe. The teenager was dragged in chains at the head of a line of Egyptian prisoners. This brutal treatment of a young girl shocked many Romans, and several influential citizens protested to Caesar. For this reason, he refrained from executing Arsinoe and later allowed her to receive sanctuary, or religious protection, in the temple of Diana, goddess of the moon and hunting.

Arsinoe's treatment was not the only result of Caesar's Egyptian conquests that many Romans found shocking. Caesar was married to a respected woman named Calpurnia, and the presence in Rome of

Cleopatra and Caesarion was considered to be an insult to the institution of marriage, which most Romans held sacred. No one mentioned the scandal openly to Caesar, of course. But Roman society abounded with gossip and some prominent people expressed their displeasure in private. One of these was the famous senator, statesman, and writer Cicero. In 44 B.C., he wrote to his friend Atticus, saying bluntly what he thought of Cleopatra, while giving her some credit for her well-known love of learning:

Marcus Tullius Cicero was one of Rome's greatest statesmen and writers. In his letters to friends he criticized Caesar and denounced Cleopatra.

I detest Cleopatra; and the voucher [spokesman] for her promises [of giving gifts of educational materials], Ammonius, knows I have good [moral] reason to do so. [However] her promises were all things that had to do with learning and not derogatory [insulting] to my dignity, so I could have mentioned them even in a public speech.[21]

Murder in the Senate

For some of Cicero's fellow senators, the open affair with Cleopatra was the least of Caesar's crimes. Already master of the Roman armies and the most powerful man in the world, Caesar had recently begun overhauling the Senate, Rome's governing body. He had expelled many senators and appointed others loyal to himself. There was even talk that he might abolish the government and declare himself king. To prevent this from happening, a group of senators, led by Brutus and Cassius, attacked Caesar in the Senate on March 15, 44 B.C. They stabbed him to death and, in tragic irony, he fell at the foot of a statue of Pompey, his old enemy. Caesar's assassination left Rome in an uproar. His close friend, the powerful general Mark Antony, stirred up public sympathy for Caesar and denounced the conspirators. Amid widespread unrest and rioting, Brutus and Cassius fled Italy.

In the meantime, Cleopatra prudently took Caesarion and sailed for Egypt, reaching Alexandria in July. With her Roman benefactor's own quest for power cut short, she was now left on her own to rule Egypt in the best way she could. Showing

Death in the Senate

The assassination of Julius Caesar on March 15, 44 B.C., was a pivotal event both for Rome and for Cleopatra. It opened up a new round of Roman power struggles and civil wars, and it robbed the Egyptian queen of her closest and most powerful supporter. The Roman historian Appian described the murder in his Roman History.

"The conspirators had left Trebonius, one of their number, to engage Antony in conversation at the door [of the Senate House]. The others, with concealed daggers, stood around Caesar like friends as he sat in his chair. Then . . . Cimber seized hold of his purple robe . . . and pulled it away so as to expose his neck, exclaiming, 'Friends, what are you waiting for?' Then first Casca, who was standing over Caesar's head, drove his dagger at his throat, but swerved and wounded him in the breast. Caesar snatched his toga from Cimber, seized Casca's hand, sprang from his chair, turned around, and hurled Casca with great violence. While he was in this position another one stabbed him with a dagger in the side. . . . Cassius wounded him in the face, Brutus smote him in the thigh, and Bucolianus in the back. With rage and outcries Caesar turned now upon one and now upon another like a wild animal, but, after receiving the wound from Brutus [his friend] he at last despaired and . . . fell at the foot of Pompey's statue. They continued their attack after he had fallen until he had received twenty-three wounds. Several of them while thrusting with their swords wounded each other."

Caesar lies dead, murdered by Roman senators.

her usual courage and fortitude, she rose to the challenge and began to concentrate her energies on domestic issues. Politically wise, she must have guessed that Rome was not finished with her and her country. And this was indeed the case. Even as she settled down on the throne her father had left her, new power struggles were brewing among the Romans, contests for world supremacy that would once again draw her into the fray.

Chapter

3 Antony and Cleopatra: The Politics of Love

During the two years following the assassination of Julius Caesar, the Roman world was in political turmoil. Into the power vacuum Caesar had left stepped three ambitious men—Antony, Caesar's longtime friend; Octavian, Caesar's eighteen-year-old grand-nephew and adopted son; and Lepidus, a popular general. They formed an alliance known as the Second Triumvirate in 43 B.C. Their aim was to "restore order" by establishing a dictatorship, in effect forcing the Roman Senate and people

To rule Rome, Marcus Aemilius Lepidus, a popular Roman general, joined forces with Mark Antony and Octavian in the Second Triumvirate in 43 B.C.

to do their bidding. And to this end they established a reign of terror. They killed many of their political opponents, including the statesman Cicero, and confiscated the money and property of several well-to-do Romans. In the meantime, Brutus, Cassius, and the other surviving conspirators, having fled to Greece, raised a large army. Their goal was to defeat the triumvirs and restore Rome's old republican government. Romans everywhere took one side or the other in preparation for all-out civil war.

In Egypt, Cleopatra watched these events closely. She realized that sooner or later Egypt would have to deal with the Romans again. Already both Roman camps were asking for Egyptian support, mainly in the form of ships, grain, and money. Cleopatra knew that the best political course was to back the party most likely to win the conflict. But at the time it was impossible to know who would be the victor. So she took the safe course. She offered both sides excuses for being unable to help them and waited to see a clear winner emerge before committing her country's resources. For example, according to Appian, "Cassius again sent to those [nations] who had rejected his application [for aid], and also to Cleopatra, queen of Egypt. . . . The queen excused herself on the grounds that Egypt was at the time suffering from famine and pestilence."[22] Cleopatra's strategy worked. She managed to stay out of the war and, by backing the winner, gained both power and prestige. In the process, whether by accident or design, she once more became entangled in a romance that had the whole world talking.

Power Struggles in Rome

In the weeks immediately following Caesar's assassination, Antony assumed most of his slain friend's powers in Rome. Antony had the support of Caesar's widow, Calpurnia, and of all Caesar's political allies, as well. Antony did not hesitate to use this support to his advantage. In Caesar's name, he appointed many public officials, all loyal to himself, recalled several people from exile, and freed others from prison. For a while, it seemed that Antony might make himself the absolute ruler that many had feared Caesar would become.

However, Antony's solo reign in Rome was short-lived. He, along with most other Romans, had severely underestimated the ambitions, intelligence, and political abilities of Caesar's adopted son, Octavian. Calling himself the "younger Caesar," Octavian arrived in Rome to claim his father's inheritance. Unknown to everyone, he also intended to acquire for himself as many of Caesar's former powers as he could. According to Plutarch, at first Antony did not take Octavian seriously. But when the young man went behind his back and gathered the support of important senators and army factions, Antony

A bust of the youthful Octavian, who at eighteen co-ruled Rome with Antony and Lepidus. He would later become Augustus Caesar, Rome's first emperor.

A Roman Tourist in Egypt

Egypt was a popular tourist attraction for Romans. And the Egyptians were eager to please their Roman guests, as evidenced by this excerpt from an Egyptian document (quoted in Life in Egypt Under Roman Rule*) sent by an official in Alexandria to the leaders of a country town.*

"Lucius Memmius, a Roman senator, who enjoys a position of great dignity and honor, is making the voyage from Alexandria . . . to see the sights. Let him be received with special magnificence, and see to it that the guest-houses are made ready at the proper places and that the landing-stages [docks] leading to them are in working order, also that the welcoming gifts . . . are presented to him at each landing-place, that the furnishings of each guest-house are ready for him, as well as the tidbits [gifts] for Petesouchos [an Egyptian crocodile god] and the [live] crocodiles, and the necessaries for viewing the labyrinth [temple maze], and the offerings for the sacrifices. And in general take the greatest pains for the visitor's complete satisfaction, and show the utmost zeal."

reluctantly had to reach an agreement with his new and formidable rival. "The young Caesar," wrote Plutarch:

Caesar's niece's son, and by testament left his heir, arrived at Rome from Apollonia, where he was when his uncle was killed. The first thing he did was to visit Antony, as his father's friend. He spoke to him concerning the money that was in his hands, and reminded him of [Caesar's legacy]. . . . Antony, at first, laughing at such discourse from so young a man, told him . . . that he wanted [lacked] good counsel [advice] and good friends to tell him the burden of being executor to [handling the estate of] Caesar would sit very uneasy upon his young shoulders. This was no answer to him [Octavian]; and, when he insisted on demanding the property, Antony went on treating him injuriously both in word and deed. . . . This made the young Caesar apply himself to [seek the help of] Cicero, and all those that hated Antony; by them he was recommended to the Senate, while he himself courted the people, and drew together the soldiers from their settlements, till Antony got alarmed, and gave him [Octavian] a meeting in the Capitol, where, after some words, they came to an accommodation.[23]

Soon afterward, Antony and Octavian joined forces with Lepidus and his troops to form a new triumvirate. All three men realized that, despite their personal differences, the alliance was, at the time, a polit-

Caesar's friend Mark Antony was, at first, the dominant member of the Second Triumvirate. Together with Octavian and Lepidus he defeated the republican army of Brutus and Cassius.

ical necessity. The conspirators were rallying their republican forces to regain control of the government, and only by uniting their powers could the three men hope to stop them.

Dividing Up the World

In the autumn of 42 B.C. the forces of Antony and Octavian converged on Philippi in northern Greece, where the army of Brutus and Cassius awaited them. Everyone involved knew that this would be one of Rome's great decisive battles. It would decide once and for all whether the future of Rome and the Mediterranean world, including Cleopatra's Egypt, lay in the hands of the Senate or in those of military dictators. "Both sides," wrote Appian,

> divined equally that this day and this battle would decide the fate of Rome completely; and so indeed it did. . . . The onset [of battle] was superb and terrible. They had little need for arrows, stones, or javelins, which are customary in war, for they did not resort to the usual maneuvers and tactics of battles, but, coming to close combat with naked swords, they slew and were slain, seeking to break each other's ranks. . . . The slaughter and the groans were terrible.[24]

Although casualties were heavy on both sides, Antony and Octavian won a decisive victory. Disgraced, Brutus and Cassius committed suicide, and any chance of restoring Rome's old republican government died with them.

The victorious triumvirs now proceeded to divide up the Mediterranean world among themselves. They considered Italy, the traditional Roman homeland, to be common, or equally shared, territory. Octavian took Spain and the large Mediterranean island of Sardinia. Lepidus took northern Africa, the region that had once been the nation of Carthage. Because Antony was considered the dominant war leader, he received the best share of all—the "east." This meant that he would control the Roman provinces in Greece, Asia Minor, and the Middle East, and also would have influence over weak independent eastern kingdoms like Egypt.

Command of the east gave Antony several clear advantages over his fellow triumvirs. First, the east was the richest part of the Mediterranean sphere, encompassing great trading centers such as Alexandria in Egypt and Antioch in Syria. That made Antony especially strong in sea power. He also had control over the eastern Roman legions, or regiments of about 5,000 men, and cavalry. This force amounted to eight legions and 10,000 horsemen, compared with three legions and 4,000 horsemen directly under Octavian's command. In addition, command of the east gave Antony the opportunity to lead campaigns against Parthia. The military leader who managed to defeat this still-potent threat to Rome would surely gain great glory and prestige.

An Unforgettable Spectacle

Control of the east also brought Antony into contact with the various Roman governors and foreign heads of state in the area, including Cleopatra. Antony had met the Egyptian queen many years before. As a young officer, he had accompanied Gabinius on the mission to rescue Auletes' throne in 57 B.C. Cleopatra was only twelve at the time, and it is unknown whether she had made any significant impression on Antony, or he on her. Now that he commanded Rome's eastern sphere of influence, he decided it was time to renew her acquaintance. He needed money, ships, and grain for his planned war with Parthia, and he reasoned that Egypt could supply him with all of these.

In late summer 41 B.C., Antony summoned Cleopatra to his headquarters at Tarsus, in the Roman province of Cilicia in southern Asia Minor. Eager to acquire his protection against Egypt's potential enemies, she gladly made the trip. Her grand arrival on a huge, ornately decorated barge was, no doubt, designed to impress Antony and the local population.

Brutus, one of Caesar's assassins, commits suicide after losing the battle of Philippi to Antony and Octavian.

The unforgettable spectacle of Cleopatra approaching in her splendid barge duly impressed Mark Antony. Plutarch's description of the event details the blaze of gold and silver, the wafting perfume, and the billowing sails of royal purple.

From Plutarch's description of the unforgettable spectacle, it is clear that she succeeded. He wrote that

> she came sailing up the river Cydnus, in a barge with gilded [gold covered] stern and outspread sails of purple, while oars of silver beat time to the music of flutes and fifes and harps. She herself lay all alone under a canopy of cloth of gold, dressed as Venus [Roman goddess of love] in a picture, and beautiful young boys, like painted Cupids, stood on each side to fan her. Her maids were dressed like sea nymphs and graces [goddesses], some steering at the rudder, some working at the ropes. The perfumes diffused themselves from the vessel to the shore, which was covered with multitudes [of local people], part following the galley up the river on ei-

ther bank, part running out of the city to see the sight.[25]

In the following weeks, Antony and Cleopatra became lovers. He was forty-one and she twenty-eight. He was married at the time to an intelligent and ambitious woman named Fulvia, his third wife. Whether he and Cleopatra were actually in love at this point is questionable. Their affair may have been politically motivated in the beginning, since each wanted something from the other. But most people did not see it this way. Appian expressed the popular sentiment, claiming that Antony "was amazed at her wit as well as her good looks, and became her [sexual] captive as though he were a young man. . . . Whatever Cleopatra ordered was done, regardless of laws, human or divine."[26] Other ancient writers, both Roman and non-Roman, echoed the same theme—that

Cleopatra had used her feminine wiles to bewitch and corrupt a noble Roman. For example, the Jewish historian Flavius Josephus called her a "wicked creature," who

was a slave to her lusts, but she still imagined that she wanted everything she could think of, and did her utmost to gain it. . . . As for Antony, he was so entirely overcome by this woman that . . . he was some way or other bewitched to do whatever she would have him [do].[27]

A Voice Like a Stringed Instrument

In his Life of Antony, *the ancient writer Plutarch recorded Antony and Cleopatra's first few days together in Cilicia in Asia Minor. Apparently, Antony was impressed with the queen's wealth, charm, intelligence, and considerable linguistic skills.*

"On her arrival, Antony sent to invite her to supper. She thought it fitter he should come to her; so, willing to show his good-humor and courtesy, he complied, and went. He found the preparations to receive him magnificent beyond expression, but nothing so admirable as the great number of lights; for on a sudden there was let down altogether so great a number of branches with [oil lamps] in them so ingeniously disposed [placed] . . . that the whole thing was a spectacle that has seldom been equalled for beauty. The next day Antony invited her to supper, and was very desirous to outdo her in magnificence . . . but he found he was altogether beaten . . . and . . . he himself was the first to jest and mock at his poverty of wit and his rustic awkwardness [crude manners in comparison to hers]. She . . . fell into it [his manner of speaking and humor] at once, without any sort of reluctance. . . . It is said . . . the contact of her presence . . . was irresistible; the attraction of her person, joining with the charm of her conversation, and the character that attended all she said or did, was something bewitching. It was a pleasure merely to hear the sound of her voice, with which, like an instrument of many strings, she could pass from one language to another; so that there were few of the barbarian nations that she answered by an interpreter; to most of them she spoke herself, as to the Ethiopians, Troglodytes, Hebrews, Arabians, Syrians, Medes, Parthians, and many others, whose language she had learnt."

But this one-sided view resulted largely from the biases of the writers. To the Romans and Egypt's Middle Eastern neighbors, Cleopatra was a wealthy foreigner to be both distrusted and envied. And it is important to note that these writers were all men who did not like the idea of a woman ruling any country. Their sexist interpretations of the events conveniently ignored the fact that Antony was a mature adult capable of making his own decisions. They also neglected to observe that he, too, hoped to gain material as well as sexual rewards from the relationship.

Living in the Lap of Luxury

Both lovers received the rewards they sought. In the fall of 41 B.C., Cleopatra agreed to supply Antony with the money and goods he needed for his Parthian campaign. In exchange, he agreed to protect her against her enemies, both domestic and foreign. To seal the bargain, he fulfilled her request that the last of her rivals for Egypt's throne be eliminated. Ptolemy XIV was already out of the way, having died two years before. But Arsinoe was still living in the temple of Diana and claiming to be the rightful queen of Egypt. Antony's henchmen soon silenced her forever.

Antony could not launch his Parthian war until spring, so he traveled with Cleopatra to Alexandria. There the lovers spent the winter enjoying one lavish feast and entertainment after another. The Greek writer Sokrates of Rhodes described one of their banquets in his work *Civil Wars*:

The service was wholly of gold and jewelled vessels [plates, cups, and so on] made with exquisite art; even the walls were hung with tapestries woven

A nineteenth-century painting depicts Antony and Cleopatra, allies as well as lovers, triumphantly entering Alexandria amidst regal splendor.

Cleopatra was famed for her wealth and extravagant life-style. More than mere self-indulgence, however, she lavished rich banquets and precious gifts on visiting foreign dignitaries, thus securing numerous political alliances by means of such royal treatment.

of gold and silver threads. . . . She invited [Antony] and his chosen friends. He was overwhelmed with the richness of the display. . . . As for the officers, each was allowed to take away the couch on which he had lain. . . . And when they went off, she supplied litters [chairs carried by slaves] for guests of high rank, with bearers. . . . The floors of the dining rooms were strewn [with roses] a cubit [twenty inches] deep, in net-like festoons spread over everything.[28]

Cleopatra's fortune, which included gold, silver, and precious gems, as well as the ample Egyptian treasury, must have been considerable to support such a luxurious life-style. Another hint of her vast wealth can be found in an account by the Roman historian Pliny the Elder of a bet she made with Antony. Supposedly, she boasted that she could spend ten million *sesterces*, prob-ably equivalent to one or two million of today's dollars, on a single meal for herself. Thinking this to be impossible, Antony took the bet. According to Pliny:

In accordance with previous instructions the servants placed in front of her only a single vessel containing vinegar, the strong rough quality of which can melt pearls. She was at the moment wearing in her ears that remarkable and truly unique work of nature. Antony was full of curiosity to see what in the world she was going to do. She took one earring off and dropped the pearl in the vinegar, and when it was melted swallowed it.[29]

Contrary to this story, vinegar does not dissolve pearls. So Pliny's sources must have been in error on this point. However, the amount of money he mentions is well in keeping with what many of Cleopatra's extravagant banquets probably cost.

Cleopatra the Thief and Murderess

The widespread prejudice against Cleopatra among the influential leaders and writers of her day was rooted first in her being a woman and second, and perhaps worse, a bold, outspoken, and ambitious woman. Jewish historian Flavius Josephus's account in his Antiquities of the Jews *was typical of those that pictured her as an evil temptress who used sex to hypnotize Antony.*

"Now at this time the affairs of Syria were in confusion by Cleopatra's constant persuasions to Antony to make an attempt upon every body's dominions [lands]; for she persuaded him to take those dominions away from their several princes, and bestow them upon her; and she had a mighty influence upon him, by reason of his being enslaved to her by his affections. She was also by nature very covetous [greedy], and stuck [stopped] at no wickedness. She had already poisoned her brother [a claim still unproven], because she knew that he was to be king of Egypt, and this when he was but fifteen years old; and she got her sister Arsinoe to be slain [a claim that *has* been proven], by the means of Antony, when she was a supplicant [worshiper] at Diana's temple at Ephesus; for if there were but any hopes of getting money, [Cleopatra] would violate both temples and sepulchres [tombs]. Nor was there any holy place that was esteemed the most inviolable [sacred] from which she would not fetch [steal] the ornaments it had in it."

Cleopatra entertains Mark Antony.

Games and Other Diversions

In addition to lavish feasts, the lovers enjoyed other diversions. According to Plutarch, Cleopatra joined with Antony in many activites normally reserved for men, such as playing dice and hunting. Certainly, Antony, used to more conservative Roman women, had never met a woman like Cleopatra. "She had at any moment," Plutarch wrote,

> some new delight or charm to meet his wishes; at every turn she was upon him, and let him escape her neither by day nor by night. She played at dice with him, drank with him, hunted with him; and when he exercised in arms [practiced fighting] she was there to see. At night she would go rambling with him to disturb and torment [play pranks on] people at their doors and windows, dressed like a servant-woman, for Antony also went in servant's disguise. . . . However, the Alexandrians in general liked it all well enough, and joined good-humoredly and kindly in his frolic and play, saying they were much obliged to Antony for acting his tragic parts at Rome and keeping his comedy for them.[30]

Antony and Cleopatra also amused themselves with outdoor activities, including fishing, of which apparently they were both fond. Plutarch related that their fishing trips often turned into elaborate practical jokes, such as the time Antony

> went out . . . to angle with Cleopatra, and, being so unfortunate as to catch nothing in the presence of his mistress, he gave secret orders to the fishermen to dive under water, and put fishes that had been already taken upon his hooks. . . . [Cleopatra, suspecting the ruse,] invited them next day to come and see him again. . . . As soon as he had let down his hook, one of her servants was beforehand with his divers, and fixed upon his hook a salted fish from Pontus. Antony, feeling his line give, drew up the prey, and when, as may be imagined, great laughter ensued, "Leave," said Cleopatra, "the fishing-rod, general, to us poor sovereigns [royalty] . . . your game is cities, provinces, and kingdoms."[31]

Antony and Cleopatra's good times came to an abrupt end early in 40 B.C. The stunning news came that Antony's wife

A Renaissance rendition of Antony and Cleopatra's feasting. The two powerful rulers were said to have partied and played jokes on each other much as any new lovers would do today.

An Eye for Real Estate

In Antiquities of the Jews, *Jewish historian Flavius Josephus claimed that Cleopatra was a greedy person who wanted everything of value she could get her hands on. And indeed, Antony used his considerable influence to secure many Middle Eastern territories for his mistress. Here, however, Josephus recalls how Cleopatra was disappointed at not being able to acquire the kingdom of Judaea, ruled by King Herod, who had once been at odds with Antony.*

"For when [Herod] was come to Antony, he soon recovered his interest [regained a good relationship] with him, by the presents he made him, which he had brought with him from Jerusalem [Judaea's capital]; and he soon induced him, upon discoursing [talking] with him, to leave off his indignation [anger] at him, so that Cleopatra's persuasions had less force [with Antony] than the arguments and presents [Herod] brought to regain his friendship: for Antony said that it was not good to require an account of a king, as to the affairs of his government, for at this rate he could be no king at all, but that those who had given him that authority ought to permit him to make use of it. He also said the same things to Cleopatra, that it would be best for her not busily to meddle with the acts of the king's government. Herod wrote an account of these things; and enlarged upon the other honors which he had received from Antony: how he sat by him at his hearing causes [public audiences], and took his diet [meals] with him every day, and that he enjoyed those favors from him, notwithstanding [in spite of] the reproaches [complaints] that Cleopatra so severely laid against him, who having a great desire of his country, and earnestly entreating [begging] Antony that the kingdom might be given to her, labored with her utmost diligence to have [Herod] out of the way; but . . . there was no longer any hope for Cleopatra's covetous [greedy] temper, since Antony had given her Coelesyria [another eastern land] instead of what she desired; by which means he had at once pacified her, and got clear of the entreaties which she made him to have Judaea bestowed upon her."

Fulvia and brother Lucius had organized a rebellion in Italy against Octavian. They knew that Antony had never really gotten along with Caesar's son, and by eliminating the young triumvir, they hoped to inspire Antony to abandon Cleopatra and return to Rome to rule all of its vast domains. But the rebellion failed. Lucius was taken prisoner, Fulvia fled to Greece, and Antony embarked immediately to meet her.

Cleopatra must have been upset at Antony's departure, for there is reason to believe that she was, by now, in love with him. She had devoted herself to him during their months together in Alexandria and she was noticeably pregnant when he left. The events that followed surely did nothing to brighten her spirits. Fulvia, who was ill when she arrived in Greece, died shortly after Antony joined her. Although Antony and Octavian were at odds, they quickly resolved their differences and in October 40 B.C. signed a document of mutual friendship known as the Treaty of Brundisium. In an added gesture of reconciliation, Antony agreed to marry Octavian's sister. Plutarch recalled:

This sister, Octavia, he [Octavian] was extremely attached to, as indeed she was, it is said, quite a wonder of a woman. Her husband, Caius Marcellus, had died not long before, and Antony was now a widower by the death of Fulvia. . . . Everybody concurred [agreed] in promoting this new alliance, fully expecting that with the beauty, honor, and prudence of Octavia . . . all would be kept in the safe and happy course of friendship. So, both parties being agreed, they went to Rome to celebrate the nuptials [wedding], the Senate [by Octavian's demand] dispensing with the law by which a widow was not permitted to marry till ten months after the death of her husband.[32]

Cleopatra had ample reason for hating Antony. He had abandoned her and married another woman. She had no way of knowing if he would ever return to Egypt or keep his promise of protecting her throne. He had also, it appeared at the time, abandoned their children. Only a few weeks after the wedding of Antony and Octavia, Cleopatra gave birth to twins, a boy and a girl, whom she later named Alexander Helios and Cleopatra Selene. Yet Cleopatra did not harbor bitterness for her Roman lover. She seemed to believe that their love was so strong that one day he would return to her. In the meantime, she had children to raise and a kingdom to rule. Drawing upon her considerable inner strengths and resources, she bravely devoted all her energies to these formidable tasks.

4 The New Isis: Cleopatra the Ruler

The weeks of Antony's absence from Egypt stretched into months and the months into years. From 40 to 37 B.C., Cleopatra guided her country alone, without the advice of Roman politicians like Caesar and Antony or ambitious regents like Pothinus. No royal rivals shared the throne, the palace, or the decision making, for her siblings were all dead. She and her children, one by Caesar and two by Antony, were all that was left of the Ptolemaic line. Perhaps at no other moment in history did a woman so completely alone face the task of administering so great a country.

Yet Cleopatra did not shrink from this task. In fact, it appears that she worked hard and ruled both fairly and competently. Records about Egypt by ancient historians and writers are scant for the years when Roman celebrities were not in residence. The everyday events and routine workings of government were not news. So when Cleopatra was not the focus of some scandal or war, few writers mentioned her or her accomplishments. However, a few references to this period in her life have survived. Contrary to the common negative stereotypes, this evidence suggests that Cleopatra was a caring, tactful, and capable ruler who managed the economy well and treated her people

justly. Two thousand years before the idea of sexual equality became recognized, she proved that a woman can govern as well as a man.

Cleopatra's likeness carved into a precious stone. Legendary love affairs and lavish life-style aside, Cleopatra proved a capable ruler of a great nation.

Cleopatra Longs for Her Lover

In his play Antony and Cleopatra, *William Shakespeare included this speech by Cleopatra, in which she, having been abandoned by Antony, wonders how he is and what he is doing in faraway Rome.*

"Where think'st thou he is now? Stands he, or sits he?
Or does he walk? or is he on his horse?
O happy horse, to bear the weight of Antony!
Do bravely, horse! for wot'st [knowest] thou whom thou
   mov'st?
The demi-Atlas of this earth [Antony and Octavian hav-
   ing divided the world between them], the arm
And burgonet [helmet] of men. He's speaking now.
Or murmuring, 'Where's my serpent of old Nile?'
(For so he calls me). Now I feed myself
With most delicious poison [bitter thoughts]. Think on
   me,
That am with Phoebus' [the sun's] amorous pinches
   [rays] black
And wrinkled deep in time? Broad-fronted Caesar,
When thou wast here above the ground [alive], I was
A morsel for a monarch; and great Pompey
Would stand and make his eyes grow in my brow;
There would he anchor his aspect [gaze], and die
With looking on his life."

A Sensible Agricultural Policy

Part of the evidence for Cleopatra's effective rule is that the Egyptian people, on the whole, were apparently satisfied with her administration of the country. This is significant when one considers how they felt about her predecessors. During most of the nearly 300 years of Ptolemaic rule, minor rebellions, riots, and tax evasion were common as the populace showed its hatred for the foreign dynasty. The Ptolemies were well known for mismanag-ing the economy and ignoring the troubles of the people. During Cleopatra's reign, however, the land was at peace. There were no rebellions, and tax collection, for the most part, proceeded normally. This change in the public attitude toward the government suggests that the Egyptians saw Cleopatra as at least a competent, if not a popular, ruler.

One of Cleopatra's policies had to have pleased her people: her successful program of improving and expanding agriculture was a foresighted move designed to build up Egypt's resources. She knew that sooner or later the Romans would again need large quantities of Egyptian grain and other foodstuffs. So accumulating large surpluses of these items would increase the political importance and net worth of the country. More food also meant lower food prices in Egypt, as well as the elimination of food shortages. These benefits almost certainly improved the government's standing with the public. In addition, to promote expanded agriculture, Cleopatra wisely lowered taxes for farmers, giving them an incentive to work hard and produce more. One of her decrees, a copy of which has survived, ordered that

> nobody should demand of [the farmers] anything above the essential Royal

An Egyptian tomb engraving shows Egyptian farmers harvesting, threshing, and storing their grain.

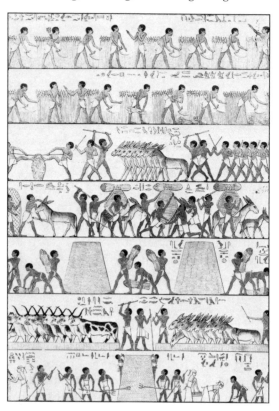

Dues [basic taxes], [or] attempt to act wrongfully and to include them among those of whom rural and provincial dues, which are not their concern, are exacted [collected]. We, being extremely indignant [about over-taxation] and considering it well to issue a General and Universal Ordinance [regulation] regarding the whole matter, have decreed that all those from the City, who carry on agricultural work in the country, shall not be subjected, as others are, to demands for *stephanoi* and *epigraphai* [types of taxes] such as may be made from time to time. . . . Nor shall any new tax be required of them. But when they have once paid the essential Dues, in kind [goods] or in cash, for cornland and for vineland . . . they shall not be molested for anything further, on any pretext whatever. Let it be done accordingly, and this put up in public, according to Law.[33]

Showing Respect for Tradition

Another reason for Cleopatra's popularity with her subjects was her practice of showing them a great deal more respect than her predecessors had. For example, she became fluent in Demotic Egyptian, the language of the country. As Plutarch pointed out, "most of the [Ptolemaic] kings, her predecessors, scarcely gave themselves the trouble to acquire the Egyptian tongue."[34] By using the native language along with Greek in the court and in official documents, she won the support of many Egyptians.

Cleopatra also went to great lengths to observe the rites of Egyptian worship, something else the preceding Ptolemies had refused to do. For centuries, the Egyptians had associated their queens with the goddess Isis, ruler of heaven and earth. Isis was also the deity who oversaw the growth and harvesting of wheat and barley, crops essential to the country's well-being. In addition, the Egyptians associated Isis with goodness and the purification and forgiveness of sins. According to tradition, the queen was the earthly representative of the goddess. At certain times, people believed, the goddess communicated to humans and accomplished various tasks through the queen's person. The cult, or religious following, of Isis extended beyond Egyptian borders. In the first century B.C. worship of the goddess was common in the Middle East, in Asia Minor, and in many other parts of the

An ancient Egyptian religious ceremony celebrating the goddess Isis as queen of heaven. The Egyptian queen traditionally personified Isis to the people. Cleopatra wisely played this role, thereby gaining the people's respect and devotion.

Mediterranean sphere, including Rome.

Cleopatra wisely took advantage of the popularity of Isis, both at home and abroad, by playing up her role as the goddess's representative. Her strong association with Isis made most Egyptians accept her even though she was Greek. Lucy Hughes-Hallet explains:

> This was a useful association for her, bridging the gap between the culture of her Greek-speaking court and that of her native Egyptian subjects. Isis was already a great deity in early pharaonic times. By linking [herself] with her and invoking her sanction and rule . . . Cleopatra [was] able to give a semblance of legitimacy . . . to the power of the dynasty, still perceived by many Egyptians as one of foreign usurpers.[35]

Cleopatra found that acting as the earthly counterpart of Isis was no small task. In order to maintain her image as the goddess's living incarnation, or spirit in bodily form, the queen had to adopt Isis's traditional dress and carriage whenever in public. On these occasions, according to Plutarch, Cleopatra was "dressed in the habit [robes] of the goddess Isis, and gave audience to the people under the name of the New Isis."[36] And she gave more than the usual number of audiences, generously reaching out to her people. In the years when Antony was away, she made appearances in many temples and villages that none of her Ptolemaic ancestors had ever bothered to visit. Often, people traveled dozens, even hundreds of miles to catch a glimpse of this mysterious New Isis as she journeyed up the Nile or through the countryside. She must have been a magnificent sight,

decked out in the goddess's traditional costume. For authenticity, she copied the outfit and hairstyle directly from ancient paintings on sacred monuments and tombs. It is likely that Cleopatra, as Isis, closely resembled the ideal description of the goddess given by the Roman writer Apuleius in his novel *The Golden Ass*:

> [Her] long thick hair fell in tapering ringlets on her lovely neck, and was crowned with an intricate chaplet [wreath] in which was woven every kind of flower. Just above her brow shone a round disk, like a mirror, or

This illustration of Cleopatra depicts her as a coy seductress, a common male image of a woman who could reduce Rome's greatest generals to lovesick schoolboys.

The Little Prince

"Cleopatra ruled Egypt alone, and brought up her three fatherless children as best she could. . . . She turned to Caesarion for comfort, which was bad for the boy. He had become prematurely adult, thrust at an early age into the role of confidant to his mother. Repeatedly, Cleopatra told him how his noble father had stood by her; how he had taken her to Rome and intended to make her the queen of a world empire. But that unreliable Antony! Why had she ever put her trust in him? Once more, Little Caesar had his mother's complete attention. Cleopatra would hardly allow him out of her sight. . . . Her beloved Caesar was dead. But he seemed to live again in his son. . . . He was nine years old in B.C. 38 and, to show the boy the country he would rule [eventually] . . . Cleopatra took him up the Nile to Dendera, where she was having a temple built dedicated to Hathor, the Egyptian goddess of love. Alighting from their *thalamegus* [houseboat], they stood looking at a wall on which workmen were carving a bas-relief of the queen, wearing the disk-and-horn headdress of Isis. In front of her was Caesarion, chatting with the gods. 'Is that me?' the boy asked. 'Well, you'd never know it.' Then back to Alexandria they went, and, after his holiday on the Nile, Little Caesar settled down to his lessons with Populos [his Greek tutor]."

like the bright face of the moon. . . . Vipers [snakes] rising from the left-hand and right-hand parting of her hair supported this disk, with ears of corn [fertility symbols] bristling beside them. Her many-colored robe was of finest linen; part was glistening white, part crocus-yellow, part glowing red and along the entire hem a woven border of flowers and fruit clung swaying in the breeze. . . . She wore [a deep black mantle] slung across her body from the right hip to the left shoulder, where it was caught in a knot resembling the boss [central ornament] of a shield; but part of it hung in innumerable folds. . . . It was embroidered with glittering stars on the hem and everywhere else, and in the middle beamed a full and fiery moon.[37]

A Thirst for Knowledge

Cleopatra also gained respect among many Egyptians for her renowned dedication to learning, especially literature, which, some ancient writers claimed, she found extremely pleasurable. Her taste in reading supposedly covered many subjects, but she was said to be particularly fond of philosophy. According to stories circulated in the centuries after her death, she carried on regular dialogues with noted philosophers of her time. No evidence survives to support this claim. However, she did financially support and often visit the Museum, a Greek center of study and learning in Alexandria. It is probable and even likely that she knew and conversed with some of the facility's gifted scientists, some of whose writings touched on philosophical themes.

According to several ancient sources, Cleopatra was a prolific and gifted writer.

Supposedly, she penned a volume on weights, measures, and coinage, another on gynecology, or feminine hygiene, and still another on alchemy, an early false-science that associated certain chemical reactions with magic. Unfortunately none of these works, if in fact they existed, survived. However, fragments of a book on cosmetics attributed to Cleopatra do exist. One of these excerpts contains advice on what to do about baldness:

> For bald patches, powder red sulphuret of arsenic and take it up with oak gum, as much as it will bear. Put on a rag and apply, having soaped the place well first. I have mixed the above with a foam of nitre, and it worked well. The following is the best of all, acting for fallen hairs, when applied with oil or pomatum; acts for falling off of eyelashes or for people getting bald all over. It is wonderful. Of domestic mice burnt, one part; of vine

A scene from an early movie about Cleopatra that starred actress Theda Bara in the title role. The Egyptian queen's interest in learning is well known. She is reputed to have written a number of works on various subjects current in her day.

*Famed actress Lily Langtry also counted Cleopatra among her many perfor-
mances. The remarkable queen of the Nile was not only pious and learned but
apparently a shrewd businesswoman as well. Her able management of Egypt's
treasury especially endeared her to her people.*

rag burnt, one part; of horse's teeth burnt, one part; of bear's grease, one; of deer's [bone] marrow, one; of reed bark, one. To be pounded when dry, and mixed with plenty of honey til it gets the consistency of honey; then the bear's grease and marrow to be mixed (when melted), the medicine to be put in a brass flask, and the bald part rubbed til it sprouts [hair].[38]

Cleopatra the Businesswoman

While Cleopatra's religious, literary, and other cultural endeavors did much to endear her to her people, what contributed most to her popularity was her wise han-

dling of the public monies. All the Ptolemies had lived lavish life-styles, largely by spending part or all of the country's treasury. Over the course of time, through the sale of grain and other means, some of the money was periodically replaced. But it was not uncommon for a ruler to run the country into debt. Cleopatra's father Auletes had certainly done so by borrowing vast sums of money from wealthy Romans. Although she herself lived as extravagantly as her predecessors, if not more so, all the while she somehow managed to keep the treasury nearly full. The extent of the wealth she accumulated was not apparent until after her death. The Egyptian treasury was so huge that when the Romans eventually took possession of it, the sudden boost to Rome's economy caused interest rates to fall from 12 to 4 percent.

Cleopatra's Kitchens

Cleopatra never ate dinner at the same hour, but still expected her food to be ready at the moment she decided she was hungry. An excerpt from Plutarch's Life of Antony *illustrates one of the indirect ways that ancient historians used to gather such information.*

"Philotas, a physician . . . who was at the time a student of medicine in Alexandria, used to tell my grandfather Lamprias that, having some acquaintance with one of the [Egyptian] royal cooks, he was invited by him, being a young man, to come and see the sumptuous [lavish] preparations for supper. So he was taken into the kitchen, where he admired the prodigious [large] variety of all things; but particularly, seeing eight wild boars roasting whole, says he, 'Surely you have a great number of guests.' The cook laughed at his simplicity, and told him there were not above twelve to sup, but that every dish was to be served up just roasted to a turn, and if anything was but one minute ill-timed, it was spoiled. 'And,' said he, 'maybe Antony will sup just now, maybe not this hour, maybe he will call for wine, or begin to talk, and will put it [eating] off. So that,' he continued, 'it is not one, but many suppers must be had in readiness, as it is impossible to guess at this hour.'"

Exactly how Cleopatra made so much money is unclear. There is no doubt that she sold some of the extra grain that resulted from her increased emphasis on agriculture. But that would not have been enough to run the country, maintain her personal spending habits, and still accumulate a large surplus. The answer may lie in special deals she made with neighboring countries and peoples. There is some evidence that she acquired valuable oil rights from Arab tribes in the Dead Sea region of Palestine. At the time, people regularly turned oil into pitch, a binding material used in building walls, roads, and ships. Oil was also used to coat mummies and to make medicines. And apparently another source of her income was King Herod of the nearby kingdom of Judaea. Although Antony had once declined to pressure Herod into ceding all Judaea to Cleopatra, he later had helped her to acquire a large tract of land near the ancient town of Jericho. This region was rich in date palms and balsam trees, from which important medicines were derived. For a hefty price, Cleopatra the clever businesswoman leased the land back to Herod. Josephus recorded that Cleopatra

passed on to Judaea; where Herod met her, and farmed [leased] of her . . . those regions about Jericho. This country bears that balsam, which is [the source of] the most precious drug that is there, and grows there alone. The place bears also palm-trees, both many in number, and those excellent in their kind. . . . As to the tributes [monies] which Herod was to pay Cleopatra for that country which Antony had given her, he [fearing Antony's wrath] acted fairly with her, as deeming it not safe for him to afford any cause for Cleopatra to hate him.[39]

A Man's Equal in Every Way

Cleopatra's successful business ventures are further evidence that she was a versatile and effective ruler who ran Egypt fairly and efficiently. Apparently, as queen she devoted her mind and energies predominantly to the task of governing. Claims made by her detractors describing her "wickedness" and constant pursuit of sexual pleasure are unfounded. All available evidence suggests that she had only two lovers in her lifetime—Caesar and Antony (her marriages to her brothers being symbolic and almost certainly never consummated). She had been faithful to Caesar until his untimely death. And despite Antony's rude treatment of her, she remained faithful to him during the years she ruled alone in Alexandria.

Cleopatra never quite gave up hope that Antony would return, for she had of-

Michelangelo planned to sculpt a bust of Cleopatra but only got as far as this preliminary sketch, now in the Louvre.

fered him a challenge that he could not easily find in Rome—a woman who was his equal in every way. Perhaps she understood that his marriage was only a political union and believed that deep down she was still the object of his passions. Her great faith and patience eventually paid off. In 37 B.C. Antony left his wife in Rome and traveled eastward to Syria to prepare for his much anticipated invasion of Parthia. The first thing he did after landing in Antioch was to send for Cleopatra.

5 Prophecy and Propaganda: Challenging the Roman Colossus

After resuming their relationship in 37 B.C., Antony and Cleopatra remained permanent allies and lovers. Their reunion and partnership significantly affected Mediterranean political affairs. From the point of view of many Romans, Antony seemed to switch his allegiance increasingly away from Rome and toward Cleopatra, so that he appeared to be abandoning his own country. Octavian and Antony had never been close, and each dreamed of ruling Rome alone. Now, Octavian saw Antony's unpopular alliance with Cleopatra as an opportunity to make his dream come true. Octavian launched a massive smear campaign against the lovers, especially Cleopatra. Designed to discredit Antony and help Octavian achieve mastery of Rome, this propaganda also succeeded in establishing a notorious and

In 37 B.C. Antony and Cleopatra renewed their love affair and their political alliance. Antony's increasing attention to Egypt's queen left him open to the intrigues of his rival Octavian, who wanted rulership of Rome all to himself.

negative image of Cleopatra that would be perpetuated through the ages.

In the meantime, Antony pursued his own dream of world dominion. A victory over the Parthians, combined with the riches of Egypt and other eastern lands, he reasoned, would give him the prestige and power to displace Octavian. Antony might then rule Rome himself, with Cleopatra as his queen. The lovers launched their own propaganda campaign, citing popular prophecies that predicted they were destined to create a better world. This bold stance put them on an inevitable collision course with Octavian. Their challenge to the colossal military might of Rome moved the Mediterranean world ever closer to the brink of war.

Driving a Hard Bargain

Antony's reasons for abandoning Octavia for Cleopatra, as they had been earlier when he left Cleopatra for Octavia, were mainly political. He had married Octavia to cement his partnership with Octavian. That move increased Antony's power and prestige in Rome's western sphere. Now he wanted to further strengthen his image as a great military leader by waging a successful war against Rome's enemy Parthia. As historian Jack Lindsay explains:

> We must realize the importance that Parthia had now assumed in Roman eyes and was to continue to hold for many centuries. Pompey had won Syria for Rome in 67 B.C.; and apart from Egypt [most] parts of the . . . east were all firmly under [Roman] control. The question was whether the ex-

pansion was to halt more or less at the Syrian frontiers or to carry boldly on over the whole area that Alexander [the Great] had conquered [much of it now ruled by Parthia]. . . . A continual tension thus existed from the days of Pompey . . . between the Roman and Parthian world.[40]

To be successful against Parthia, Antony needed Egyptian money, foodstuffs, and ships. Although he probably loved Cleopa-

Mark Antony, with Cleopatra's help, hoped to gain dominion of Rome by conquering the Parthians.

This detail of a painting by seventeeth-century Italian master Giovanni Tiepolo depicts Cleopatra, dressed like an Italian duchess of his own time, disembarking from her barge.

tra and wanted to get to know his children by her, their new partnership was, at least at first, mostly a matter of smart military strategy.

And though Cleopatra was, no doubt, overjoyed that Antony had returned to her, she had her own political agenda to promote. She was determined that this time, no matter how the relationship developed, she would get her fair share of power and prestige. So she drove a hard bargain with Antony. She agreed to supply him with the materials he needed for the Parthian campaign and to build a fleet to

protect his eastern realm. In exchange, she demanded that he give her control over extensive territories in Palestine and southern Asia Minor.

Antony agreed, and they sealed the bargain by resuming their sexual relationship. The two spent the winter of 37 B.C. together in Antioch. The following spring, Antony departed with his eastern Roman legions to begin his war with Parthia, once more leaving Cleopatra pregnant.

Antony Humiliated

The Parthian campaign and the events that immediately followed it profoundly affected Antony's image and determined the direction of his subsequent political affairs, including his alliance with Cleopatra. The war he had hoped would make him an epic hero proved a costly failure. Finding it too difficult to transport his siege equipment overland, he had to abandon it. Then, one of his allies betrayed him and joined the Parthians. Finally, some surprisingly effective Parthian tactics, combined with military blunders by Antony's own officers, resulted in embarrassing Roman defeats. Plutarch described one situation in which a Roman officer became separated from the main body of the army while the enemy closed in from the rear:

> On the fifth day, Flavius Gallus, a brave and active officer, who had a considerable command in the army, came to Antony, desiring of him some light infantry out of the rear . . . Which when he had obtained, he beat the enemy back . . . maintaining his

own ground, and engaging boldly. The officers who commanded in the rear, perceiving how far he was getting from the body of the army, sent to warn him back, but he took no notice of them. . . . Gallus, charging the enemies in the front, was encompassed by a party that fell upon his rear. . . . In this engagement were killed three thousand [Romans], five thousand were carried back to the camp wounded, amongst the rest Gallus, shot through the body with four arrows, of which wounds he died.[41]

Eventually, Antony had to abandon the campaign. He reached Syria near the end of 36 B.C. with only slightly more than half of the troops he had started with.

This humiliating situation seriously hurt his standing with Romans everywhere.

Antony soon faced a fateful decision. Cleopatra arrived in Syria in January 35 B.C., shortly after giving birth to their third child, whom she had named Ptolemy Philadelphus. The Egyptian queen brought money and fresh clothes for Antony's troops. Not long afterward, news came that Octavia was on her way with supplies and troops to reinforce her husband, and Antony now had to choose between the two women. For reasons that remain unclear, he sent word to Octavia, ordering her to return to Rome. Perhaps now that his embarrassment in Parthia had damaged his reputation and partially humbled him, he was motivated more by love for Cleopatra than by politics.

Antony's ill-fated war with the Parthians was disastrous for Rome and for his own political ambitions.

Standing Up for Roman Honor

Of the many propaganda speeches Octavian gave against Antony and Cleopatra, some have been preserved in the Roman History *of the Greek historian Dio Cassius. In this excerpt, Octavian calls his troops to uphold Rome's honor and tradition in the coming war by not allowing a mere woman to defeat them.*

"Soldiers, there is one conclusion that I have reached, both from the experience of others and at first hand: it is a truth I have taken to heart above all else, and I urge you to keep it before you. This is that in all the great enterprises of war, or indeed in human affairs of any kind, victory comes to those whose thoughts and deeds follow the path of justice and reverence for the gods. No matter what the size and strength of our force might be . . . still I base my confidence far more upon the principles which are at stake in this war than upon the advantage of numbers. We Romans are rulers of the greatest and best parts of the world, and yet we find ourselves spurned and trampled upon by a woman of Egypt. This disgraces our fathers, who defeated Pyrrhus, Philip of Macedon, Perseus, and Antiochus [all former Roman enemies]. . . . It disgraces our own generation, who have conquered the Gauls [northern barbarians], . . . marched as far as the Danube and beyond the Rhine [rivers in central Europe], and crossed the sea to Britain. The men who achieved these feats of arms I have named would be cut to the heart if ever they knew that we have been overcome by this pestilence of a woman."

Whatever his reasons, this marked the great turning point of Antony's career. By siding with Cleopatra, a foreigner, against Rome, he appeared to be turning his back on his countrymen.

Outrage in Rome

In the following two years, Antony's partnership with Cleopatra continued to hurt his reputation and weaken his ties with Rome. Octavian took full advantage of this seemingly reckless behavior. The propaganda campaign he launched played on and heightened the indignation and resentment of many Romans, who felt that Antony was insulting and demeaning them when he started dressing like an Egyptian and adopting Egyptian customs. It also angered them that he, a mighty Roman general, seemed to have stooped to doing a woman's bidding, and a woman with a scandalous reputation at that. According to Dio Cassius:

An artist's conception of Rome, the Eternal City, as it might have looked in Antony and Cleopatra's time. Romans feared Antony would hand the government of Rome over to Cleopatra.

She had, it was believed, enslaved him so completely that . . . she was saluted by him as "queen" and as "mistress," and she had Roman soldiers [his men] in her bodyguard, all of whom had her name inscribed upon their shields. She visited the market-place with Antony . . . [following] on foot together with her eunuchs. He also . . . carried an Oriental dagger in his belt, wore clothes which were completely alien to Roman custom, and appeared in public seated upon a gilded couch or chair. Painters and sculptors depicted him with Cleopatra, he being represented as Osiris [Egyptian god of the afterlife] . . . and she as . . . Isis, and it was this practice more than anything else which gave the impression that she had laid him under some spell and deprived him of his wits.[42]

What upset many Romans even more was the rumor, amply exploited by Octavian, that Antony was plotting with Cleopatra to take over Rome's eastern lands. Its western lands might also be in jeopardy. In fact, this was probably more than just a rumor. Antony and Cleopatra appeared to be building themselves a new image, one that pictured them and their children as supreme rulers. In 34 B.C. they staged a spectacular ceremony known as the Donations of Alexandria, in which Antony proclaimed Cleopatra Queen of Kings. He also declared young Caesarion to be King of Kings. In addition, Antony publicly granted several eastern Roman territories to his Egyptian children, something he had no legal right to do. Dio Cassius wrote that

> the Romans were so outraged by these disclosures [reports] that they were willing to believe that other rumors current at the time were equally true, namely that . . . [Antony] would hand over the city of Rome to Cleopatra and transfer the seat of government to Egypt. Public hostility became so intense that not only Antony's enemies . . . but even his closest friends utterly condemned his action.[43]

Antony and Cleopatra are hailed as the divine Osiris and Isis, ruling deities of Egypt.

A Leader for the Golden Age

While Roman resentment against them increased, Antony and Cleopatra countered with their own brand of propaganda. Hers was nonverbal. It consisted of using her considerable financial resources to stage lavish public spectacles. Her grand entrance on the barge when she met Antony in Tarsus had been one of them. Now, she appeared often in magnificent religious ceremonies, always wearing the splendid robes of Isis and accompanied by musicians, soldiers, and adoring crowds. Such shows were designed to advertise her wealth and power, to make it clear to her enemies that she was a force to be reckoned with. The Romans who witnessed or heard about these spectacles got the message.

Antony's propaganda was of a different sort. He attempted to boost his public image by openly claiming descent from the legendary Greek hero Hercules, who most Romans assumed had really existed. Plutarch explained that Antony had a

> very good and noble appearance . . . giving him altogether a bold, masculine look that reminded people of the faces of Hercules in paintings and

sculptures. It was, moreover, an ancient tradition that the Antonys were descended from Hercules, by a son of his called Anton; and this opinion [Antony] thought to give credit to.[44]

The most effective use of propaganda by Antony and Cleopatra was the manipu-lation of ancient prophecies to bolster their prestige. For hundreds of years, priests and writers in various Mediterranean lands had foretold the coming of a golden age, a new world order in which wars and crime would be eliminated and happiness would reign. Usually, these sto-

Antony: A Firsthand Description

In his Life of Antony, *as in his other works, Plutarch drew upon writings by eyewitnesses who had seen and talked with his subject. These ancient sources no longer exist, but it is probable that this description of Antony is reasonably accurate.*

"He had also a very good and noble appearance; his beard was well grown, his forehead large, and his nose aquiline [pleasingly curved], giving him altogether a bold, masculine look that reminded people of the faces of Hercules [the Greek hero] in paintings and sculptures. It was, moreover, an ancient tradition, that the Antonys were descended from Hercules, by a son of his called Anton; and this opinion he [Antony] thought to give credit to by the similarity of his person just mentioned, and also by the fashion of his dress. For, whenever he had to appear before large numbers, he wore his tunic girt [belt] low about the hips, a broadsword on his side, and over all a large coarse mantle [an outer robe meant to make him look more impressive]. What might seem to some very insupportable [unacceptable], his vaunting [bragging], his raillery [teasing], his drinking in public, sitting down by his men as they were taking their food, and eating, as he stood, off the common soldiers' tables, made him the delight and pleasure of the army. In love affairs, also, he was very agreeable: he gained many friends by the assistance he gave them in theirs, and took other people's raillery upon his own with good-humor. And his generous ways, his open and lavish hand in gifts and favors to his friends and fellow-soldiers, did a great deal for him in his first advance to power, and after he had become great, long maintained his fortunes."

ries predicted that a special person, often associated with the sun, would emerge to lead the new world. Until his death and the demise of his empire, many people had believed that Alexander the Great was the prophesied new leader. In 40 B.C., Virgil, the most famous poet in Rome, composed his *Fourth Eclogue*, a poem that repeated the theme of the coming golden age. Virgil wrote:

> The Last Age . . . is at hand;
> the great cycle of ages begins afresh. . . .
> Down from high heaven is sent a new progeny [child].
> On the Boy soon to be born, who'll end the Race
> of Iron [the present age] and make the Race of Gold [bathed in the sun's rays] rise up. . . .
> He'll share the Life of the Gods; Heroes he'll see
> mingled with Gods, himself beheld by them:
> he'll rule the peaceful Earth with his father's Virtues.[45]

Virgil's poem was widely popular. But the references in it to the coming world and new leader were general and often vague. So various individuals and groups interpreted this version of the prophecy in different ways, attempting to make it fit their own particular circumstances. In the following century, for example, the early Christians insisted that Virgil was predicting the birth of Jesus of Nazareth and the coming of a Christian world.

In fact, Virgil, a close friend of Octavian's, had written the poem to help legitimize the Treaty of Brundisium, the political deal Octavian and Antony struck in 40 B.C. Since Antony had married Octavian's

The Roman poet Virgil wrote of a coming golden age ruled by Antony and Octavia's offspring. But it was not to be so.

sister, the "progeny" of the union would carry the blood of the two most powerful triumvirs. According to this shrewd combination of prophecy and propaganda, the son of Antony and Octavia would rule over a new and better Roman world. Unfortunately for Octavian, Octavia, and Virgil, however, Antony spoiled the prediction by siding with Cleopatra and shunning Rome.

Antony and Cleopatra proceeded to use Virgil's poem to their own advantage. Apparently, Cleopatra had been planning to do so for some time. It had not been by accident that she had named her and Antony's first son Alexander Helios. Both names were associated with the prophesied new leader—Alexander alluding to Alexander the Great and Helios being a Greek sun god. Had not Virgil predicted greatness for Antony's son? Cleopatra sim-

A Theatrical Piece of Insolence

Antony's ceremony, the Donations of Alexandria, angered many Romans. In his Life of Antony, *Plutarch described the controversial spectacle.*

"The division he made among his sons at Alexandria [was very unpopular]; it seemed [to most Romans] a theatrical piece of insolence and contempt of his country. For assembling the people in the exercise ground, and causing two golden thrones to be placed on a platform of silver, the one for him and the other for Cleopatra, and at their feet lower thrones for their children, he proclaimed Cleopatra queen of Egypt, Cyprus, Lybia, and Coelesyria, and with her conjointly [sharing power] Caesarion, the reputed son of the former Caesar, who left Cleopatra with child. His [Antony's] own sons by Cleopatra were to have the style of king of kings; to Alexander [Helios] he gave Armenia and Media, with Parthia, so soon as it should be overcome [conquered]; to Ptolemy [Philadelphus], Phoenicia, Syria, and Cilicia. Alexander was brought out before the people in Median costume, the tiara [crown] and upright peak [hat], and Ptolemy, in boots and mantle [cloak] and Macedonian cap done about with the diadem [crown]; for this was the habit of the successors of Alexander [the Great], as the other was of the Medes and Armenians. . . . Cleopatra was, as at other times when she appeared in public, dressed in the habit [costume] of the goddess Isis."

ply implied that she, and not Octavia, was the mother of the boy in the prophecy. Antony, now at odds with Octavian, went along with this idea. He and Cleopatra made the boy a symbol of the new world they wanted to build in place of the one dominated by Rome. And in so doing they gained considerable support in the east. Many people in the region hated the Romans and were willing to back any leader strong enough to stand up to Rome.

To Save or Ruin the World?

Not surprisingly, Octavian and his supporters found all this bold posturing by their eastern adversaries both disquieting and threatening. So Octavian stepped up his propaganda attacks, especially against Cleopatra. He called her a harlot, or prostitute, and a deceitful and treacherous creature. These attacks were so effective

Cleopatra's womanhood was what ultimately threatened the Romans, who could not accept that a woman could rule as ably as a man.

that they permanently tarnished Cleopatra's image. More than a century later, for instance, the Roman writer Valleius Paterculus stated as a matter of fact that Octavian had fought "to save the world," while Cleopatra had fought "to ruin it."[46] Many other later judgments of the Egyptian queen were just as unkind and equally untrue.

By 33 B.C., the rift between Octavian and Antony and Cleopatra had grown dangerously wide. Both sides realized that war was inevitable and both began making preparations. In the meantime, Octavian justified the idea of war to the Roman people by continuing to denounce his opponents. He asked:

> Who would not tear his hair at the sight of Roman soldiers serving as bodyguards of this queen? . . . Who would not weep when he sees and hears what Antony has become? . . . He has abandoned his whole ancestral way of life, has embraced alien and barbaric customs. . . . And to crown it all, he bestows gifts of whole islands and parts of continents as though he were master of the entire earth and sea. . . . In the end, I cannot describe to you any greater prize than that of . . . preserving the proud tradition of your native land, of punishing those who have rebelled against us, of conquering and ruling over all mankind, and of allowing no woman to make herself equal to a man.[47]

Octavian's meaning was only too clear. Cleopatra was a threat to Roman pride and honor, a threat that must be eliminated.

6 Battle for the World: The Showdown at Actium

For nearly two years, the opposing armies of the east and west prepared for the struggle that would decide the fate of the Mediterranean world. In the west stood Octavian, now the most powerful man in Rome. Octavian and Antony, suspecting Lepidus of plotting against them, had dropped the third man from the triumvirate a few years earlier. And by siding with Cleopatra against Rome, Antony had forfeited his own triumviral title. That left Octavian as the sole triumvir. Although the three-man alliance was now dead, he retained all of its official powers, which he fully intended to use in defeating Antony and imposing his will on Rome.

A movie scene depicts Roman legions gathering in front of the Senate building as they prepare to go to war against Antony and Cleopatra.

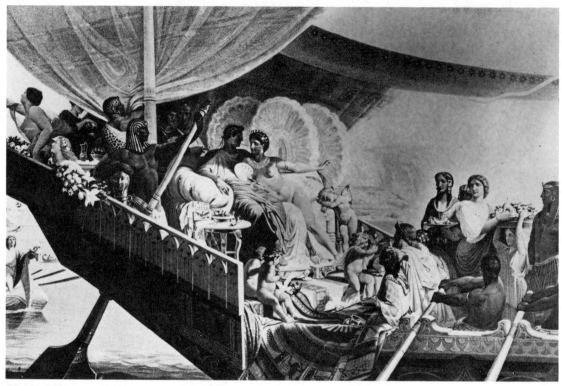

The biased image of Cleopatra as a sexual temptress is clearly seen in this Renaissance painting where she, nude, reclines with Antony on her barge. In reality, no queen would ever so appear in public.

On the other side stood Antony and Cleopatra. Though they faced the strongest nation on earth, they had good reason to believe that they could achieve victory. Antony still held the loyalty of large numbers of Roman troops in the east, and several eastern lands promised to send him troops and ships. He also had Cleopatra's money and ships, both of which were considerable assets. And despite widespread hatred for Antony in the west, some powerful men in Rome still supported him. In the spring of 32 B.C., to Octavian's dismay, the city's two consuls, or chief administrators, and about three hundred senators, fully one-third of the Senate, fled Rome and joined Antony. Thus, the leaders on

both sides were confident of winning the coming fight for world supremacy. It likely surprised many when what promised to be a long and drawn-out contest was decided by the results of a single battle.

Octavian Seizes the Initiative

Antony and Cleopatra were so confident of victory that they took their time drawing their plans against Octavian. Their overall strategy was to build up their land and sea forces in Asia Minor and Greece, and then invade Italy. In 33 B.C. they traveled to Ephesus on the coast of Asia Minor and began to assemble their fleet. War preparations continued in the coming months. In the meantime, the lovers made leisurely visits to the Greek island of Samos, the city of Athens, and other locations in the region. They held elaborate festivals and ceremonies at each stop, to advertise their prestige and power. To gain a further propaganda advantage, they enlisted the aid of well-known Greek athletes, musicians, and actors, whose public praises would win them increased popularity. To gain this support, Antony issued an edict promising to better the status of such performers. The edict granted them exemption from military service, complete immunity from liturgies [having to serve in public office without pay], freedom from billeting [having to house soldiers], and . . . a truce and personal security, and the right to wear purple [the color worn only by senators and royalty].[48]

But taking so much time to increase their prestige was not necessarily Antony and Cleopatra's wisest strategy. Their failure to take the initiative and attack Italy immediately may have cost them the war. In 33 B.C. Octavian was still struggling to raise enough money and troops to mount

A Gentler, Kindlier Octavian

Octavian, who later became Augustus, the first Roman emperor, was a shrewd politician who could be both brutal and ruthless, as his attacks on Cleopatra testify. However, in his Lives of the Twelve Caesars, *written after Augustus's death, the historian Suetonius emphasized a tamer, kindlier image of Octavian/Augustus.*

"[He] never made war on any nation without just and due cause, and he was so far from desiring to increase his dominion [power] or military glory at any cost, that he forced the chiefs of certain barbarians to take oath in the temple of Mars the Avenger [god of war] that they would faithfully keep the peace for which they asked. . . . On those who rebelled often or under circumstances of especial treachery he never inflicted any severer punishment than that of selling the prisoners, with the condition that they should not pass their term of slavery in a country near their own, nor be set free within thirty years. The reputation for prowess [skill] and moderation which he thus gained led even the Indians and the Scythians, nations known to us only by hearsay, to send envoys of their own free will and sue for his friendship and that of the Roman people. The Parthians, too, readily yielded to him . . . and at his demand surrendered the standards [battle flags] which they had taken from Crassus and Mark Antony."

his offensive. At the time, he might not have been able to repel a major assault. As it happened, however, his adversaries' delays gave him the time he needed to build up his forces. According to Plutarch:

> The speed and extent of Antony's preparations alarmed Caesar [Octavian], who feared he might be forced to fight the decisive battle that summer. For he wanted [lacked] many [military] necessaries, and the people grudged very much to pay the taxes [needed to purchase them]; freemen being called upon to pay a fourth part of their incomes, and freed slaves an eighth of their property, so that there were loud outcries against him, and disturbances throughout all Italy. And this is looked upon as one of the greatest of Antony's oversights, that he did not then press [proceed with] the war. For he allowed time at once for Caesar to make his preparations and for the commotions [in Italy] to pass over. For while people were having their money called for, they were mutinous and violent; but, having paid it, they held their peace.[49]

Still, in sheer numbers Octavian's forces never matched Antony's. Octavian had about 400 ships, carrying a total of about 37,000 armed soldiers, and about 80,000 land troops. On the other hand, as Jack Lindsay explains:

> Antony's fleet . . . now held eight squadrons [groups] of the line (each 60 ships); one squadron was led by Cleopatra's flagship. . . . Over 500 ships in all, with 125,000 to 150,000 men as crews. He had set himself to outbuild Octavian in size of ship. The largest ships had belts of squared iron-bound timber to prevent ramming, powerful beaks [bow rams], and heavy catapults mounted on deck-towers. . . . On land Antony had nineteen legions . . . 60,000 to 65,000 tough soldiers, with light-armed men, mostly Asian, perhaps 70,000 to 75,000. . . . Of cavalry he had about 12,000 [men]. . . . That Cleopatra could feed and supply such a large host shows her great resources.[50]

But what Octavian lacked in numbers, he made up for in other ways. First, he had a talented, shrewd, and experienced admiral named Agrippa commanding his fleet. Antony, a general, had no experience in marine warfare, and his own naval commanders were no match for Agrippa. Octa-

Roman military leader Marcus Agrippa led Octavian's naval forces against Antony and Cleopatra in 31 B.C.

The trireme, with its three banks of oars, was the typical battleship used in Roman times. In such ships Agrippa engaged Antony and Cleopatra's navy at Actium.

vian also gained an important strategic advantage by launching the first offensive. Instead of waiting in Italy for Antony to come to him, early in 31 B.C. he began advancing his forces on Greece. At the time, Antony and Cleopatra's forces were still disorganized, parts of their fleet being stationed at various ports dotting the southern coast of Greece. In March, Agrippa boldly seized the port of Methone, one of Antony's most important naval bases. From there, Agrippa's ships raided other ports in the area and partially disrupted Antony's supply lines. At the same time, Octavian marched his land troops into southern Greece. He stopped and established a large camp near the port of Actium, located at the mouth of a wide gulf.

The Decision to Fight at Sea

Seeking to stop Octavian's advance, Antony and Cleopatra traveled to Actium a few days later and set up their own camp only a few miles from their opponent's. This, however, proved to be a costly mistake. In a series of brilliant, lightning raids, Agrippa completely cut off Antony's supply lines from the south. It quickly became clear to Antony and Cleopatra that they were trapped at Actium. The Roman fleet blocked escape from the gulf in the south, and Octavian's troops controlled the land routes to the north. The lovers had to face the fact that Octavian, despite his smaller forces, had outmaneuvered them and now held the advantage. There was nothing left to do but fight.

The question was whether to engage the Romans on land or at sea. Antony's chief officer, Canidius Crassus, favored giving up the fleet and attacking Octavian's land troops. He argued that while Agrippa was a formidable admiral, Antony was a gifted general and had a good chance of defeating Octavian. Anyway, said Canidius, "it would be simply ridiculous for Antony, who was by land the most experienced commander living, to make no use of his well-disciplined and numerous infantry,

Size Is No Match for Courage

Before the battle of Actium, many Roman soldiers and sailors were no doubt worried about the great size of the ships of Antony and Cleopatra. To quell these fears, Octavian gave his men a morale-boosting speech, part of which Dio Cassius preserved in his Roman History.

"You must not imagine that the size of their ships or the stoutness of their timbers is any match for our courage. What ship has either killed or wounded any by its own efforts? I believe that their height and their solid construction will make them more difficult for their rowers to keep under way, and less responsive for their helmsmen to steer. What use can ships like these be to the fighting-men aboard when they can attack neither head-on nor abeam [from the side], the two maneuvers which you know are essential in naval warfare? I do not suppose that they intend to use infantry tactics against us at sea, nor are they thinking of shutting themselves up behind wooden walls and inviting a siege, so to speak, since it could only be to our advantage if we were faced with an immobile wooden barrier. If their ships remain motionless, as if they were moored there, we can rip them open with our rams, or else bombard them from a distance with our siege engines [catapults], or burn them to the water's edge with our incendiary [flaming] missiles. On the other hand, if they do venture to move, they will be too slow either to overtake or to escape our vessels: their weight makes them too cumbersome to cause damage to us, and their size makes them most liable to suffer it themselves."

scattering and wasting his forces by parcelling them out in the ships."[51]

Antony agreed with Canidius but Cleopatra did not. According to Plutarch, she forcefully argued in favor of a sea battle and managed to win Antony over to the idea. "Cleopatra prevailed [won the argument] that a sea-fight should determine all."[52] But while she undoubtedly favored using the fleet, having spent so much Egyptian money building and sup-

plying it, it is unfair to blame her fully for this fateful decision. Octavian had his opponents trapped, and without fresh supplies they would grow weaker with time. It became clear that he intended to wait, keep his distance, and refuse a land fight. That left Antony little choice. As scholar Ernle Bradford put it:

Plutarch, who was writing about one hundred years later . . . naturally enough [given the lasting effect of Octavian's propaganda] puts the blame for the events of Actium entirely upon the shoulders of Cleopatra. . . . But the fact of the matter was that so long as Octavian refused to accept a land engagement Antony was powerless. The decision was accordingly taken to prepare for a break-out [of the trap] by sea.[53]

Corpses on the Waters

The naval encounter at Actium, one of the most decisive events of ancient times, took place on September 2, 31 B.C. In the morning, the opposing land armies filed onto the beaches to watch the struggle.

Before the battle began, both Antony and Octavian visited contingents of their

The chaos and destruction of the battle of Actium is captured in this drawing of the great naval battle. Agrippa's strategy won the day for Octavian as his smaller, more maneuverable ships bested the more powerful, but clumsier, Egyptian vessels.

This painting of the battle of Actium shows the tight quarters in which the ships had to maneuver. Such conditions favored the smaller Roman ships.

respective forces, partly to make sure that all was in readiness, and also to build their soldiers' morale. According to Plutarch:

> Antony in a small boat went from one ship to another, encouraging his soldiers, and bidding them stand firm and fight as steadily on their large ships as if they were on land. The masters [captains] he ordered that they should receive the enemy lying still as if they were at anchor, and maintain [control over] the entrance of the port, which was a narrow and difficult passage. Of Caesar [Octavian] they relate that, leaving his tent and going round, while it was yet dark, to visit the ships, he met a man driving an ass, and asked him his name. He [the man] answered him that his own name was "Fortunate, and my ass," says he, "is called Conquerer." And afterwards, when he [Octavian] disposed [placed] the beaks [rams] of the ships in that place in token of his victory, the statue of this man and his ass in

bronze were placed amongst them. After examining the rest of his fleet, he went in a boat to the right wing, and looked with much admiration at the enemy lying perfectly still in the straits.[54]

At first, the opposing fleets held their positions. At least an hour or two passed while the soldiers on shore waited anxiously for the vessels to engage each other. Eventually, a strong sea breeze blew in. Taking advantage of the sudden wind, the Egyptian ships began to advance across the gulf and, as Dio Cassius recorded:

> The fleets came to grips and the battle began. Each side uttered loud shouts to the men aboard, urging the troops to summon up their prowess [skills] and their fighting spirit, and the men could also hear a babel of orders being shouted at them from those on shore.[55]

According to Dio, the two sides had different strategies. Antony's strategy was to shoot large volleys of stones and arrows at the enemy vessels as they approached. If his troops damaged a Roman ship in this manner, they would attempt to entrap it by grabbing it with iron grappling hooks. His soldiers would then cross over to the other ship and engage the enemy in fierce hand-to-hand combat. Sometimes Antony's vessels were successful. But often they were not and many, their hulls pierced by battering rams on the bows of the Roman ships, sank quickly. Thousands of Antony and Cleopatra's rowers and soldiers drowned and some of their corpses floated on the waters, obstructing the rowers on both sides.

On the other hand, Octavian's strategy was to use the great size of Antony's ships against him. The Roman ships, smaller and lighter than Antony's, could speed around and ram their opponents at will. If they could not sink a vessel, they would pull back and then suddenly attack again. Or they would seek out a different ship and try to ram it over and over. The Romans, Dio wrote,

> feared their adversaries' . . . long-range missiles . . . so they . . . would sail up suddenly so as to close with their target before the enemy's archers could hit them, inflict damage . . . and then quickly back away out of range. Octavian's ships resembled cavalry, now launching a charge, and now retreating, since they could attack or draw off as they chose, while Antony's were like heavy infantry, warding off the enemy's efforts to ram them.[56]

Plutarch's account of the battle agrees, saying that "the engagement resembled a land fight, or, to speak yet more properly, the attack and defense of a fortified place; for there were always three or four vessels of Octavian's [hovering] about one of Antony's."[57]

Defeat and Disgrace

For hours the battle raged, with casualties mounting on both sides. It is doubtful whether Cleopatra, commanding a squadron of some sixty ships, had actually been involved in the fighting up to this point. It appears that part of her and Antony's strategy was for these vessels to keep their distance from the action and guard her flagship. It carried a large portion of her gold and jewels, treasure they would need to carry on the war.

Suddenly, at the height of the battle, Cleopatra ordered her ships to retreat. "Cleopatra's sixty ships," said Plutarch, "were seen hoisting sail and making out to sea in full flight, right through the ships that were engaged [in the battle]."[58] Antony soon followed her with some of his own ships. Before leaving, he ordered his remaining vessels to cover the retreat by launching an all-out attack on the Romans. Bravely, Antony's men followed his orders. But they were soon overwhelmed. In desperation, Dio wrote, they "forced their attackers back with boat-hooks, cut them down with axes, hurled down stones and other missiles . . . and engaged all who came within reach."[59] Despite the valor of Antony's remaining troops, it was no use. With Antony and Cleopatra gone, the battle was lost and the surviving crews grudgingly surrendered the following day.

The lovers' flight played directly into Octavian's hands. Their escape not only

Cleopatra directs her naval troops from her ship during the battle of Actium.

commander or a man. . . . For as if he had been born part of her, and must move with her wheresoever she went, as soon as he saw her ship sailing away, he abandoned all that were fighting and spending their lives for him.[60]

To Fight Another Day

In reality, however, Antony, an experienced military leader who deeply cared about his men, had not acted out of cowardice. The evidence suggests that the lovers had planned their escape all along. They were trapped at Actium with little hope of victory, and the best course seemed to be to forfeit one battle in order to survive long enough to eventually win the war. To win, they needed money. Therefore, their retreat with the treasure gave them the means to fight on. Ernle Bradford wrote that "The romantic version as projected first by Plutarch . . . is clearly not true. . . . Antony's conduct can hardly be considered very noble, but it was practical. He had lost the battle of Actium . . . but he still had a chance to fight another day."[61]

Indeed, both sides recognized that the struggle was far from over. For Octavian, history seemed to be repeating itself. His father, Julius Caesar, had vanquished a mighty Roman in Greece and pursued him to Egypt. Now Octavian found himself acting out the same drama. With high hopes, his quarry, Antony and the woman known to many as the Queen of Kings, sailed the remains of their once-mighty fleet toward Egypt and an uncertain destiny.

ensured him victory, it also seemed to prove what he had been saying all along about his adversaries. Running away and leaving Antony to die, Octavian maintained, confirmed that Cleopatra was a treacherous character without decency or honor. And Antony's cowardly abandonment of his own troops showed that he was still hopelessly bewitched by her. Plutarch later summed up the Roman opinion of Antony's disgrace:

> Here it was that Antony showed to all the world that he was no longer . . . a

7 In Death Unconquered: The Last Days of a Proud Queen

After their defeat at Actium, Antony and Cleopatra hoped to continue the struggle against Octavian. They planned to regroup their land forces, use her treasure to build a new fleet, and launch a new offensive. According to Dio Cassius, "They continued to make arrangements to carry on the war in Egypt both at sea and on land, and for this purpose they summoned all the neighboring tribes and rulers who were on friendly terms to come to their help."[62]

But almost immediately their plans began to fall apart. Shortly after the remains of Antony's fleet surrendered at Actium, his land troops did the same. This deprived him and Cleopatra of an essential part of their military strength. Cleopatra was still rich enough to raise more troops from her eastern neighbors, but one by one her and Antony's former allies deserted them. They were now seen as losers who had no real chance against Rome. Few wanted to risk incurring Octavian's wrath by backing them. Typical was the reception Antony received late in 31 B.C. when he traveled to Cyrene, a small kingdom located west of Egypt, to collect troops to defend Egypt. The local ruler coldly killed his messengers and refused him aid. Antony and Cleopatra finally saw that they were alone. Their dreams of a new Mediterranean world order had been dashed and, with Octavian sure to follow them to Egypt, their future appeared grim.

Octavian the conqueror. The victorious Octavian returned to Rome before pursuing Antony and Cleopatra to Egypt.

This painting illustrates Act 4, Scene 10, of Shakespeare's play Antony and Cleopatra.

A Hopeless Situation

Octavian did not advance on Egypt immediately, however. Hearing about a political crisis in Italy that needed his attention, he headed for Rome, putting off his Egyptian campaign for a few months. Apparently, he realized that Antony and Cleopatra could no longer find military backing and that he could afford to take his time in punishing them. During these months the mood in Alexandria was somber. Feelings of anxiety and doom were common in the streets, in military camps, and in the palace. Sooner or later, everyone knew,

Roman sails would appear on the horizon and Egypt would be at Octavian's mercy.

Antony and Cleopatra each reacted differently to the obviously hopeless situation. Antony became moody and depressed. Once he had been one of the most powerful men in the world and had looked forward to a bright and glorious future. Now he was beaten and humiliated, a traitor in the eyes of his countrymen.

Cleopatra, on the other hand, displayed her characteristic strength and boldness in the face of adversity. At first, she turned to pompous ceremony, as she had in the past, to keep up her public image as an all-powerful queen. Dio wrote that "she had the ships' prows hung with garlands, as though she had actually won a victory, and had songs of triumph chanted to the accompaniment of flute players."[63] But this approach failed to impress or soothe her sad and fearful subjects.

Later, Cleopatra boldly tried to avert impending disaster by buying Octavian off. She sent him expensive gifts, asking him to let her live and later, after her death, to allow her sons to reign in Egypt.

"Cleopatra sent to Octavian," Dio recalled,

a golden scepter [royal staff], a golden crown, and the royal throne of Egypt, signifying that through these gifts she was offering him the kingdom as well. . . . She hoped that even if Octavian regarded Antony as a mortal enemy, he would take pity on her [and her children] at least.[64]

Octavian accepted her gifts but promised

A Queen and Her Plotting Gang

With the possible exception of Hannibal, the Carthaginian who invaded Italy in the third century B.C., the Romans hated Cleopatra more than any other foreign ruler. Not surprisingly, they were happy when they received the news of her death. Horace, one of Rome's most popular poets, captured this sentiment in his poem "Fatal Creature" from his Odes.

"Now is the time to drink, with feet released
to beat the earth, and gratefully to spread,
   my friend, with Salian [wild and uncontrolled] feast
   each god's reclining-bed [in general, to celebrate].
Till now we dared not raid the ancestral rack
for Caecuban. A queen [Cleopatra] had planned in hate
   to smash the [Roman] Capitol and sack
   the conquered Roman state.
She and her plotting gang, diseased and vile,
went mad with heady dreams of baseless pride:
   drunk with their luck [successful] were they awhile,
   but soon the frenzy died [they were defeated]. . . .
Seeing her ruined court with placid eyes,
she grasped the asps [poisonous snakes] and did not
   feel the pains,
   wishing the venom to surprise
   and brim at once her veins.
For brooding arrogance had nerved [made bolder] her
   thought.
She grudged [did not want] in triumph-shackles
   [chains] to be seen,
   [or] by the Liburnian galleys [luxurious Roman
      barges] brought
   to slavery, a queen."

to pardon her only if she killed Antony. This, of course, she refused to do. Desperate, Antony also attempted to bribe Octavian, offering to kill himself if it would save Cleopatra's life. Curiously, since he had already indicated his desire to see Antony dead, Octavian completely ignored this noble gesture.

Desertion and Surrender

Eventually, the much-dreaded Roman sails appeared on the horizon. Octavian landed his army several miles east of Alexandria in July 30 B.C. and advanced on the city. Antony, the hardened soldier, shook off his depression and bravely led his small remaining loyal cavalry and infantry forces against the foe. To the surprise of many, at first he was successful. According to Dio, Antony "marched to face Octavian before Alexandria. His cavalry fell upon the enemy when they were exhausted from their [march along the coast] and scored a success." But in a subsequent infantry attack, Antony's soldiers were badly defeated. He then tried to bribe Octavian's troops. "He had shot arrows into Octavian's camp," Dio continued, "which carried leaflets promising the soldiers six thousand *sesterces* each." But this desperate move quickly backfired.

Octavian of his own accord read out [loud] the leaflets to his soldiers and did his utmost to counter their effect, on the one hand to incite feelings of shame at the treachery they were be-

A Roman cavalryman dispatches his opponent in battle. Roman soldiers were well-trained and very loyal. Octavian's appeal to his men's loyalty overcame any temptation they might have had to accept Antony's bribe to desert Rome.

Choosing the Right Poison

It is sometimes difficult for modern scholars to separate fact from fiction in ancient sources. In this excerpt from his Life of Antony, *Plutarch describes Cleopatra killing people to test poisons. Most modern historians find this unlikely and attribute the story to the Roman rumor and propaganda mill.*

"Cleopatra was busied in making a collection of all varieties of poisonous drugs, and, in order to see which of them were the least painful in the operation, she had them tried upon prisoners condemned to die. But, finding that the quick poisons always worked with sharp pains, and that the less painful were slow, she next tried venomous animals, watching with her own eyes whilst they were applied, one creature to the body of another. This was her daily practice, and she pretty well satisfied herself that nothing was comparable to the bite of the asp, which, without convulsion or groaning, brought on a heavy drowsiness and lethargy, with a gentle sweat on the face, the senses being stupefied [dulled] by degrees; the patient, in appearance, being sensible of no pain, but rather troubled to be disturbed or awakened like those that are in a profound natural sleep."

ing invited to commit, and on the other to arouse enthusiasm for his own cause. In the end, the very episode itself stirred his men's emotions: they were angry at the attempt to undermine their loyalty and were anxious to prove that they did not deserve to be regarded as traitors.[65]

The next day brought Antony and Cleopatra still closer to the brink of ruin. Antony had hoped to assemble the Egyptian ships in Alexandria's harbor for an attack on Octavian's vessels. But at the last moment the Egyptian captains surrendered their ships to the Romans. Seeing that it was pointless to fight on against impossible odds, Antony's remaining land troops then deserted him and surrendered, too. It is unclear whether Cleopatra ordered her ships to surrender. If she did, she probably was trying to be practical and avoid any further loss of Egyptian men and ships. In any case, Antony believed she had given the order and he was, understandably, angry. Fearing his wrath, she hid, along with three of her maid servants, inside an elaborate tomb that she had been building for herself for some time.

A Heartbreaking Scene

Alexandria was in chaos. The fleet was in enemy hands, the Romans were entering the city, and the queen was nowhere to be found. The streets were filled with people, some running for the imagined safety of their homes, others fleeing toward the countryside. In the midst of all this confusion, someone wrongly informed Antony that Cleopatra was dead. As Plutarch described it:

> He, believing it, cried out, "Now, Antony, why delay longer? Fate has snatched away the only pretext [reason] for which you could say you desired yet to live." Going into his chamber, and there loosening and opening his coat of armor, "I am not," said he, "troubled, Cleopatra, to be at present

bereaved of [grieving for] you, for I shall soon be with you."[66]

Determined to take his life, Antony asked one of his personal attendants, a man named Eros, to stab him. But Eros, caring too much for Antony to do the deed, drew his sword and, in a fit of emotion, turned the weapon upon himself. According to Plutarch, as the man fell dead at his feet, Antony said:

> "It is well done, Eros . . . you show your master how to do what you had not the heart to do yourself." And so

Italian painter Pompeo Battoni captured the poignancy of Antony's death in the arms of his beloved Cleopatra. The love that ruled their lives in the end perhaps prevented them from ruling the world.

he ran himself into the belly [with his own sword], and laid himself upon the couch. The wound, however, was not immediately mortal; and the flow of blood ceasing when he lay down, presently he . . . entreated [begged] those [servants] that were about him to put him out of his pain; but they all fled out of the chamber, and left him crying out and struggling.[67]

Soon some of Cleopatra's servants appeared and carried Antony out. Cleopatra had heard about her lover's attempted suicide and she was determined that he not die alone. At her orders, the servants bore Antony to her tomb. Fearing that if she unlocked the doors the Romans might gain access to the structure, she and her maids threw down ropes, which the servants on the ground tied around Antony. Plutarch recorded the heartbreaking scene that followed:

> Those that were present say that nothing was ever more sad than this spectacle, to see Antony, covered all over with blood and just expiring [almost dead], thus drawn up, still holding up his hands to her, and lifting up his body with the little force he had left. . . . And Cleopatra, with all her force, clinging to the rope, and straining with her head to the [stone window sill], with difficulty pulled him up, while those below encouraged her with their cries, and joined in all her efforts and anxiety. When she had got him up, she laid him on the bed, tearing all her clothes, which she spread upon him; and, [in grief] beating her breast with her hands, lacerating [cutting] herself, and disfiguring her own face with the blood from his wounds,

she called him her lord, her husband, her emperor.[68]

Antony was not an emperor. Nor was he Cleopatra's husband, for they had never formally married. Yet she had pledged to love and support him for as long as they lived and now, in this moment of his greatest need, she was fulfilling that pledge. A little while later he died in her arms.

A Deed Done Quickly and Well

Not long after Antony's death, Octavian found out where Cleopatra was hiding and sent soldiers to capture her. When they broke into the tomb, she tried to stab herself but they restrained her and brought her to Octavian. The "treacherous creature" who had caused him so much trouble for so long was finally in his custody. He kept her well guarded, for he wanted to take her back to Rome alive. There, as Caesar had done with her sister Arsinoe, Octavian would display Cleopatra, bound in chains, in his victory triumph.

After a few days, Octavian paid Cleopatra a visit. He mistakenly believed his own propaganda and saw her as a greedy woman, interested only in maintaining her personal pleasures and possessions. So he offered to let her keep her jewels and other tokens of treasure. Apparently, he was convinced this would pacify her long enough for him to transport her to Rome as his victory prize. But while Octavian was wily, Cleopatra skillfully used her own considerable talents at deceit. Though she was, no doubt, still thinking about suicide, she hid this plan and made him believe he had outsmarted her. Plutarch described this meeting of two master manipulators:

Some few days later, Caesar [Octavian]

Cleopatra and Octavian

Not long after Antony's death, Octavian visited Cleopatra in her quarters. This is Plutarch's version of the incident, from his Life of Antony.

"Some few days later, Caesar [Octavian] himself came to make her a visit and comfort her. She lay then upon her pallet-bed in undress and, on his entering, sprang up from off her bed, having nothing on but the one garment next [to] her body, and flung herself at his feet, her hair and face looking wild and disfigured, her voice quivering, and her eyes sunk in her head. The marks of the blows she had given herself [while Antony was dying] were visible about her bosom, and altogether her whole person seemed no less afflicted than her soul. But, for all this, her old charm, and the boldness of her youthful beauty, had not wholly left her, and, in spite of her present condition, still sparkled from within, and let itself appear in all [her] movements. . . . Caesar, desiring her to repose herself [relax], sat down by her; and, on this opportunity, she said something to justify her actions, attributing what she had done to the necessity she was under, and to her fear of Antony; and when Caesar, on each point, made his objections, and she found herself confuted [contradicted], she broke off at once into language of entreaty [begging]. . . . And at last, having by her a list of her treasure, she gave it into his hands. . . . Caesar was pleased to hear her talk thus, being now assured that she was desirous to live. And, therefore, letting her know that the things [treasures] she had laid by [presented] she might dispose of as she pleased, and his usage of her should be honorable above her expectation, he went away, well satisfied that he had overreached [gotten the better of] her, but, in fact, was himself deceived."

Cleopatra pretends to beg for her life from Octavian.

her, and . . . still sparkled from within, and let itself appear in all [her] movements. . . . She broke off at once into language of entreaty [begging]. . . . And at last, having by her a list of her treasure, she gave it into his hands. . . . Caesar was pleased to hear her talk thus, being now assured that she was desirous to live. And, therefore, letting her know that the things [treasures] she had laid by [presented] she might dispose of as she pleased, and his usage of her should be honorable above her expectation, he went away, well satisfied that he had overreached [gotten the better of] her, but, in fact, was himself deceived.[69]

Eventually, Cleopatra discovered Octavian's plan to take her to Rome and pub-licly display her in his triumph. Determined to rob her captor of the satisfaction of her humiliation, she secretly plotted her own death. One day while visiting her tomb she managed to shake off her guard by asking him to take a letter to Octavian. Then she and two faithful servants, Charmion and Iras, locked themselves in. "Crowning the tomb with garlands and kissing it," wrote Plutarch, "she gave orders to prepare her a bath, and, coming out of the bath, she laid down and made [ate] a sumptuous meal."[70] Afterward, the other women brought her two asps, highly poisonous snakes, and she pressed them to her breast. The potent snake venom coursed through her blood.

In the meantime, Octavian had read the letter. When he saw that it was a request that Cleopatra be buried with

A Fictional Enactment

Modern novelist Martha Rofheart picked up where Plutarch left off by creating realistic dialogue for Cleopatra and Octavian. Although no one will ever know for sure, this scene from Rofheart's novel The Alexandrian *may be a fairly accurate reconstruction of the real incident.*

"Octavian looked as though his mother still made his clothes, in the country; they were awkwardly draped and frayed at the hem, gray from poor washing. He was small-built, as I remembered him from long ago, almost to the point of delicacy. . . . His every move was crisp and measured; his eyes were cold as gems.

He wagged his finger at me, his thin smile a mockery of great Caesar's. . . . 'You have been a bad girl, Cleopatra. . . . Why have you spoiled your looks? Your Caesar is displeased.' And he reached out to cup my chin, placing his mouth on mine. His lips were cool and hard. . . . I nearly spat. . . .

'I have been ill, sir. . .'

'You may call me Octavian,' he said, inclining his head. . . . He cleared his throat. 'I have a list here,' he said, snapping his fingers, and taking it from the soldier who held it, 'a list of the royal assets—plate, coins, gold bars, electrum [mixture of gold and silver], silver, jewels . . .' He ran his eye quickly down the scroll. . . . 'These things [jewelry]—' and he pointed to them on the scroll, 'they are still worn sometimes?'

'Oh, always,' I said. 'The queen is no queen without them.'

'Well, my dear, queen you shall be—for one last time. . . . You must wear them all—all the royal jewels. I will give them into your keeping. . . . And they shall stay with you . . .'

'I should not like to be their death,' I said, sadly, but with honey [lies] upon my lips.

'My dear,' he said . . . 'they shall not die—no more than you! . . . Caesar will have his own [chance to sleep with Cleopatra] . . . like his uncle before him.'

I . . . said, softly, 'You do me too much honor, oh, August one. . . . I fear I shall disappoint you, Octavian.'

'My dear,' he said slyly . . . 'how can that be? You— the greatest courtesan [prostitute] in the world!'"

Antony, he realized what she was doing and dispatched some soldiers to stop her. But it was too late. "The thing had been quickly done," Plutarch continued, and,

> on opening the doors, they saw her stone-dead, lying upon a bed of gold, set out in all her royal ornaments. Iras, one of her women, lay dying at her feet, and Charmion, just ready to fall, scarce able to hold up her head, was adjusting her mistress's diadem [crown]. And when one that came in said angrily, "Was this well done of your lady, Charmion?" "Extremely well," she answered [proudly], "and as became [befitted] the descendant of so many kings"; and as she said this, she fell down dead by the bedside.[71]

Octavian had taken almost everything from Cleopatra—her throne, her country, and her lover. But he could not capture her dignity, and in death her proud spirit remained unconquered.

The Game of World Power

The deaths of Antony and Cleopatra left Octavian the most powerful man in the world. The powers of the triumvirate, the command of Rome's vast empire, the allegiance of the armies, and the riches of Egypt—all were his now. And he made full use of his powers. First, he promptly executed Caesarion, ensuring that the boy would never, as Caesar's son, claim a share of Roman power. Octavian also put to death Antony's son by Fulvia, since the heir of a former triumvir might one day make a similar claim. Antony's children by Cleopatra, whom Octavian apparently did not regard as a threat, were spared. In a surprisingly merciful gesture, considering how he felt about their mother, he even saw to it that they had a good upbringing. He also honored Cleopatra's last request by allowing her to be buried alongside her beloved Antony. Octavian was less merci-

Octavian discovers, too late, that Cleopatra intended suicide after all.

The Wealth of Egypt

When the Romans annexed Egypt as a province in 30 B.C. they acquired the country's considerable wealth, some of which they simply took from Egyptian citizens. In his Roman History, *Dio Cassius told how this was accomplished.*

"Great quantities of treasure were found in the palace. . . . Heavy fines were also collected from all who were charged with any misdemeanor [crime]. Apart from these, all the rest, even though no specific accusation could be brought against them, were required to surrender two-thirds of their property. These resources were used to provide all the [Roman] soldiers with the pay that was due to them, and those who were serving with Octavian at that time received a further thousand *sesterces* on condition that they did not plunder [loot] the city. All those who advanced loans to Octavian's cause were repaid in full, and both the senators and the knights [cavalry officers] who had taken part in the war received large sums of money. In all the Roman Empire gained greatly in wealth and its temples in ornaments."

ful with Cleopatra's subjects. Later, in 30 B.C., he officially annexed Egypt, making it a Roman province. Because Egypt was the last of the independent Hellenistic kingdoms to fall to Rome, this marked the end of Greek rule in the Mediterranean.

After returning to Rome, Octavian continued to consolidate his power. By 27 B.C., he had managed to eliminate nearly all traces of support for the old republican government. The Senate gave him the name Augustus, or "the great and exalted one," and from that time on, he ruled the Roman world as its first emperor.

Augustus lived to be seventy-five, and in his long career he had many rivals and enemies, nearly all of them men. But none caused him more trouble or threatened his authority more boldly than his one female rival—Cleopatra. In her thirty-nine years, twenty-one of them as Egypt's queen, she had shown intelligence, skill, and ambition. And she had demonstrated the sheer courage and audacity to make herself one of the great players in the male-dominated game of world power. In the end, she lost that game, but not before leaving her mark on Rome and on history. Without meaning to, Dio Cassius left her a fitting epitaph when he wrote, "Through her own unaided genius she captivated the two greatest Romans of her time, and because of the third, she destroyed herself."[72]

8 A Woman for the Ages

Cleopatra's character and deeds were already legendary when she was living, and after her death her legend continued to grow. She became a kind of mythical character whose colorful life and tragic death captured and excited generation after generation. The fascination with her character and exploits has remained constant through the ages and constitutes her unique legacy.

This fascination with Cleopatra has many dimensions. Many people have been drawn to her sexual persona, her image as an irresistible charmer who seduced and manipulated the greatest men of her day. Others have focused on the more mystical aspects of her personality. In this context, she is seen as a mysterious figure, assuming the guise of a supreme goddess (Isis) and delving into the strange religious secrets of the exotic east. The romantics of every century have viewed Cleopatra as history's most sublime lover, a woman ruled by her passions who sacrificed herself for the love of a man. The most popular modern view of her, on the other

The Romans find Cleopatra dead in her tomb. Her abiding sense of dignity impelled her to choose death by her own hand rather than submit to Octavian's planned humiliation of her in Rome.

A carving in the Egyptian temple at Dendera of Cleopatra wearing the mystic crown of Isis.

tion on earth. In a sense, then, as a character who has captured the imaginations of millions, Cleopatra was not one, but many women.

These many Cleopatras have been the subjects of numerous histories, poems, paintings, songs, operas, plays, novels, and films. In fact, so many literary and artistic versions of her exist that simply listing them would fill at least one volume of this size. These diverse works picture her in every possible light. Some, such as *De claris mulieribus* by the fourteenth-century Italian poet Giovanni Boccaccio, depict her as greedy and cruel. Other works take the opposite approach. The fourteenth-century English writer Geoffrey Chaucer wrote a poem describing Cleopatra as a "good woman," both loyal and virtuous. Her physical descriptions are equally varied. Painters of the European Renaissance usually pictured her as a slightly overweight blond. This was because at the time plump women were considered attractive and the most socially accepted racial features were Caucasian, or light-skinned. By contrast, a number of twentieth-century writers and painters have depicted Cleopatra as a black African. These and many other versions of her have conveniently ignored that in fact she was Greek, with dark hair and a swarthy complexion.

Cleopatra in Literature

The first well-known literary versions of Cleopatra were the references to her in Greek, Roman, and Jewish histories that appeared in the first and second centuries A.D., not long after her death. One of the most important of these was Plutarch's

hand, is that of liberated woman. This version of her story emphasizes how she, a woman alone in a man's world, ruled a country and challenged the mightiest na-

Antony and Cleopatra feasting. Innumerable artists have depicted Cleopatra's many-sided personality in innumerable ways.

Lives of the Noble Grecians and Romans. Others were Dio Cassius's *Roman History,* Appian's work of the same title, Flavius Josephus's *Antiquities of the Jews,* and Suetonius's *Lives of the Twelve Caesars.* These works dutifully chronicled the main events of her life. But they tended also to mix rumors and popular propaganda stories with the facts. So, even in its first two centuries, the Cleopatra legend was already a colorful combination of the real and the romantic.

Many other literary versions of the legend appeared in the centuries that followed. One of the most important was by the tenth-century Arab historian Al Masudi. Like other Arab writers, Masudi wrote of the greatness of Greek civilization and the brilliance of its artists, thinkers, and scientists. So his picture of Cleopatra, the last great Greek ruler, emphasized her talents in these areas. According to Masudi, she was

> a princess well versed in the sciences, disposed to the study of philosophy and counting scholars among her intimate friends. She was the author of works on medicine, charms, and other divisions of the natural sciences. These books bear her name and are well known among men conversant [familiar] with art and medicine.[73]

Another popular work that depicted Cleopatra as intelligent was the 1757 novel *The Lives of Cleopatra and Octavia* by

English writer Sarah Fielding. Here, the Egyptian queen is smart, sophisticated, and independent, a foreshadowing of the image popular today—that of the liberated woman.

Many other literary works have tended to treat Cleopatra far less kindly. Typical were *Zim-Zizimi*, an 1858 poem by the renowned French writer Victor Hugo, and English writer H. Rider Haggard's 1889 novel *Cleopatra*. Both depict Cleopatra as wicked and bloodthirsty. They also strongly emphasize her image as a *femme fatale*, or a woman who destroys men by seducing them. This was a character type very popular in nineteenth-century literature, and Cleopatra, in many people's minds, was history's prime example of a seductress. These and the many other works that showed her in a negative light were obviously strongly influenced by Plutarch, Appian, and Dio Cassius.

The Height of Romanticism

Perhaps the most popular literary versions of the Cleopatra legend have been stage plays. Among the many were *Antony and Cleopatra* by sixteenth-century playwright Don Celso Pistorelli and *Antony and Cleopatra: A Tragedy* by seventeenth-century English playwright Sir Charles Sedley. Both versions are highly romantic and colorful. In Pistorelli's, Antony has a dream in which Cleopatra turns into a snake and wraps herself around him. Sedley's play portrays her as being so blindly devoted to Antony that she kills herself because she thinks it will please him.

Without doubt, the most famous plays about Cleopatra are William Shakespeare's tragedy, *Antony and Cleopatra*, written in 1607, and George Bernard Shaw's 1900 work *Caesar and Cleopatra*. Shakespeare derived his plot and character information largely from Plutarch's *Lives*. As a result, the ancient author's biases, which color his subject as a person of low moral character, are retained in the play. Thus, Shakespeare's Cleopatra is often greedy, jealous, vain, and selfish. Yet Shakespeare added other dimensions to her character—versatility, ageless beauty, and a deep and sincere love for Antony. In this play, the romantic vision of a great woman dying for love reaches its height. In her highly emotional death scene, she worships the memory of her dead lover, saying:

A Renaissance painting of Cleopatra depicts her as a contemporary woman, yet wearing an asp—her instrument of suicide—as a necklace.

I dreamt there was an Emperor Antony.
O, [give me] such another sleep, that I might see
But such another man. . . .
His face was as the heav'ns, and there-in [in it] stuck
A sun and moon, which kept their course and lighted
The little o [globe], th' earth. . . .
His legs bestrid [stood over] the ocean: his reared arm
Crested [covered] the world: his voice was propertied
As all the tuned spheres [music of the heavens]. . . .
In his livery [cloak]
Walked crowns and crownets [small crowns]: realms and islands were
As plates dropped from his pocket. . . .
Think you there was or [ever again] might be such a man
As [to compare with] this I dreamt of?[74]

Shaw's delightful comedy-drama views Cleopatra in a different light. He did not closely follow the ancient sources, relying more on his own imagination in creating characters and situations. His Egyptian queen is first seen as a frightened young girl hiding from the Romans beneath a stone Sphinx. Caesar happens by and, not realizing who he is, she warns him to watch out for the monstrous Romans. She has heard that they all have tusks and tails, and that they eat people. In the course of the story, Caesar helps her transform her-

This engraving of Cleopatra grieving over the dying Antony is from a scene in Shakespeare's Antony and Cleopatra *performed at London's Drury Lane Theatre where the bard staged most of his works.*

From the very beginning of the genre, filmmakers, like other artists, wanted to portray the life of Cleopatra. This 1917 silent version starred Theda Bara as Cleopatra and Fritz Leiber as Caesar.

self into a strong, brave, and capable young queen. And as he leaves for Rome in the end, he promises to send her another Roman, one "brisk and fresh, strong and young, hoping in the morning, fighting in the day, and revelling [playing] in the evening."[75] This was Shaw's way of foreshadowing her coming love affair with Antony.

Cleopatra as Artists Saw Her

A favorite in the artistic world as well as the literary, Cleopatra has been the subject of hundreds of paintings, musical compositions, and films. In one of the most famous paintings, the renowned sixteenth-century Italian artist Michelangelo showed her wrapped in serpents and with snakes for hair. This was a reference to the asps with which she reportedly ended her life. Some of the other well-known paintings of Cleopatra are by Giacomo Francia (Italian, fifteenth century), Sir Joshua Reynolds (English, eighteenth century), Jean-Baptiste Regnault (French, eighteenth century), Jean Gérôme (French, nineteenth century), and Frederick Sandys (English, nineteenth century).

One of the most notable musical versions of Cleopatra is German-English composer George Frideric Handel's 1724 opera *Julius Caesar*. This piece, like many literary works of the 1700s and 1800s, portrays the queen in a romantic manner. She openly expresses her heartfelt love and respect for Caesar, whom she looks up to as a guide and protector. As in most works relating to Cleopatra, Caesar takes on a heroic stature. Among the many other musical pieces inspired by Cleopatra are the opera *The Death of Cleopatra* (1806) by Italian composer Antonio Sografi and a popular song by nineteenth-century French composer Hector Berlioz.

Of all the various art forms, film is perhaps the most versatile, influential, and popular. When movies were introduced in the late 1800s and early 1900s, it became possible for the first time to show living, moving versions of famous historical personages. From the beginning, one of the most popular of these film subjects was Cleopatra. No fewer than six silent films about her and her exploits were produced before 1930. The most famous of these was the 1917 epic *Cleopatra*, starring Theda Bara, a widely loved actress of the day.

Of the many sound films made about Cleopatra, by far the two most spectacular were the versions made in 1934 and 1963.

The first, directed by Cecil B. DeMille, starred Claudette Colbert as Cleopatra, Warren William as Caesar, and Henry Wilcoxon as Antony. DeMille concentrated on lavish production values, crowding the screen with huge sets and thousands of extras. One of the most effective scenes is the queen's arrival in Tarsus on her royal barge, which authentically reproduces Plutarch's classic description of the event. Colbert's Cleopatra is both charming and coldly calculating.

Director Joseph L. Mankiewicz's later

A scene from Cecil B. DeMille's 1934 Cleopatra, *starring Claudette Colbert as the Egyptian queen and Henry Wilcoxon as Antony. The film was typical of DeMille's lavish productions.*

Cleopatra's Extravagance Lingers On

Nearly everything about the real Cleopatra was larger than life and extravagant. The same thing can be said for modern film versions of her life, especially the 1963 version, directed by Joseph Mankiewicz and starring Elizabeth Taylor, Richard Burton, and Rex Harrison. In this excerpt from his book The Ancient World in the Cinema, *film historian Jon Solomon explains why the movie ran way over budget and ended up costing $62,000,000.*

"Bad weather in London and Rome [where many scenes were filmed], excessive prices charged by the Italians, and other delays and costs added daily figures onto the growing budget. At one point, elephants were hired for the famous scene in which Cleopatra enters Rome in a magnificent show. The elephants ran loose and disrupted the shooting. Mankiewicz ordered the beasts off the set and called them "wild." Fox [Twentieth-Century Fox, the studio making the film] was then sued for $100,000 for "slandering" the elephants! To build the Alexandria exteriors, a beach at Anzio [in Italy] was rented. Rental alone cost $150,000. By the end of shooting, the weary production manager became a laughing stock; he turned frugal at the wrong time in the wrong way. He told the cast, "Save on the paper cups." Miss Taylor's hairdresser was earning eight hundred dollars per week. Her chauffeur was also making extraordinary amounts of money. Rex Harrison became insulted since his chauffeur was making less; "Why the hell should Elizabeth Taylor's chauffeur get more than mine just because she has a bigger chest!" [Harrison reportedly said]. Another big reason for the great expense was the panic caused by the upper echelon [top executives] of Twentieth-Century Fox. "Hurry up," they insisted. Mankiewicz was forced to rewrite the script over the weekends and to shoot the film in historical sequence [the real order of events] in the following week. No film is ever shot in this way. Unused actors cost the same amount of money as used ones, and 250 days of shooting add up; Taylor was receiving $50,000 per week, Harrison $10,000. Then one day, 1,500 spears were "lost" somehow. Once, the Italian locals delivered an $80,000 bottled-water bill to Fox. Liz calculated that to average two and one-half gallons of water per person per day! Someone was outfoxing Fox."

Elizabeth Taylor as Cleopatra in the 1963 film epic that cost $62 million. According to some critics, Taylor had difficulty portraying Cleopatra's complex character.

version was the most expensive movie produced up to that time. Counting the amount spent to distribute it worldwide, it cost a staggering $62,000,000, more than twenty times the cost of an average film of its day. The movie was heavily advertised. Pictures of its stars—Elizabeth Taylor as Cleopatra, Rex Harrison as Caesar, and Richard Burton as Antony—graced the largest billboard in the world in New York City. Although the film is overlong and sometimes slow-moving, it presents a colorful and fairly accurate view of the first-

century Mediterranean world. The film's most visually impressive scenes are Cleopatra's spectacular entrance into Rome and the sea battle of Actium. Taylor's portrayal of the legendary queen, while not great acting, is acceptable, considering the difficulty of the part. As film historian Jon Solomon explains:

> Taylor has a particularly difficult part to play. She must be a beautiful queen, an ambitious politician, a soft woman, a determined mother. . . . It is perhaps too much to ask of an actor or actress that he or she completely find the character of one of the most complicated people in history.[76]

Larger than Life

Indeed, it is Cleopatra's complexity, the idea that she was a brilliant combination of many women, that has fascinated people through the centuries. Perhaps no one film, or painting, or poem, or book will ever fully capture her multifaceted personality or her bold spirit. But it is certain that writers and artists will continue to try. Once she was flesh and blood, as mortal as anyone else. But in legend she became *im*mortal. Cleopatra the legend lived, loved, and died in a manner larger than life, and for that she is likely to remain a uniquely compelling woman for the ages.

Notes

Introduction: Fact Versus Fiction

1. Quoted in Lucy Hughes-Hallett, *Cleopatra: Histories, Dreams and Distortions.* New York: HarperCollins Publishers, 1991.
2. Dio Cassius, *Roman History*, translated by Ian Scott-Kilvert. New York: Penguin Books, 1987.
3. Hughes-Hallett, *Cleopatra.*

Chapter 1: Egypt and Rome: The World of Cleopatra's Childhood

4. Naphtali Lewis, *Life in Egypt Under Roman Rule.* Oxford, England: Clarendon Press, 1983.
5. Lionel Casson, *Daily Life in Ancient Egypt.* New York: American Heritage, 1975.
6. James Henry Breasted, *Ancient Times: A History of the Early World.* Boston: Ginn and Company, 1944.
7. Agatharchides, quoted in Casson, *Daily Life in Ancient Egypt.*
8. Lewis, *Life in Egypt Under Roman Rule.*
9. Strabo, *Geography*, quoted in Jack Lindsay, *Cleopatra.* London: Constable and Company, 1970.
10. Casson, *Daily Life in Ancient Egypt.*
11. Plutarch, *Lives of the Noble Grecians and Romans*, translated by John Dryden. New York: Random House, 1932.
12. Plutarch, *Lives.*

Chapter 2: Caesar and Cleopatra: The Quest for Power

13. Julius Caesar, *War Commentaries of Caesar*, translated by Rex Warner. New York: New American Library, 1960.
14. Caesar, *War Commentaries.*
15. Appian, *Roman History*, translated by Horace White. Cambridge, MA: Harvard University Press, 1964.
16. Caesar, *War Commentaries.*
17. Plutarch, *Lives.*
18. Appian, *Roman History.*
19. Lucan, *Pharsalia*, quoted in Lindsay, *Cleopatra.*
20. Suetonius, *Lives of the Twelve Caesars*, translated by J. C. Rolfe. Cambridge, MA: Harvard University Press, 1964.
21. Cicero, *Letters to Atticus*, translated by E. O. Winstedt. Cambridge, MA: Harvard University Press, 1961.

Chapter 3: Antony and Cleopatra: The Politics of Love

22. Appian, *Roman History.*
23. Plutarch, *Lives.*
24. Appian, *Roman History.*
25. Plutarch, *Lives.*
26. Appian, *Roman History.*
27. Flavius Josephus, *Antiquities of the Jews*, in *The Works of Flavius Josephus*, translated by William Whiston. Edinburgh, Scotland: William P. Nimmo, no date given.
28. Sokrates, *Civil Wars*, quoted in Lindsay, *Cleopatra.*
29. Pliny the Elder, *Natural History*, translated by H. Rackham. Cambridge, MA: Harvard University Press, 1967.
30. Plutarch, *Lives.*
31. Plutarch, *Lives.*
32. Plutarch, *Lives.*

Chapter 4: The New Isis: Cleopatra the Ruler

33. Quoted in Lindsay, *Cleopatra.*
34. Plutarch, *Lives.*
35. Hughes-Hallett, *Cleopatra.*

36. Plutarch, *Lives*.

37. Apuleius, *The Golden Ass*, quoted in Hughes-Hallet, *Cleopatra*.

38. Quoted by George Bernard Shaw in his Notes to *Caesar and Cleopatra*. Baltimore: Penguin Books, 1951.

39. Josephus, *Antiquities of the Jews*.

Chapter 5: Prophecy and Propaganda: Challenging the Roman Colossus

40. Lindsay, *Cleopatra*.

41. Plutarch, *Lives*.

42. Dio Cassius, *Roman History*.

43. Dio Cassius, *Roman History*.

44. Plutarch, *Lives*.

45. Virgil, *Fourth Eclogue*, quoted in Lindsay, *Cleopatra*.

46. Valleius Paterculus, *Compendium of Roman History*, quoted in Hughes-Hallett, *Cleopatra*.

47. Quoted in Dio Cassius, *Roman History*.

Chapter 6: Battle for the World: The Showdown at Actium

48. Quoted in Lindsay, *Cleopatra*.

49. Plutarch, *Lives*.

50. Lindsay, *Cleopatra*.

51. Quoted in Plutarch, *Lives*.

52. Plutarch, *Lives*.

53. Ernle Bradford, *Cleopatra*. New York: Harcourt, Brace, Jovanovich, 1972.

54. Plutarch, *Lives*.

55. Dio Cassius, *Roman History*.

56. Dio Cassius, *Roman History*.

57. Plutarch, *Lives*.

58. Plutarch, *Lives*.

59. Dio Cassius, *Roman History*.

60. Plutarch, *Lives*.

61. Bradford, *Cleopatra*.

Chapter 7: In Death Unconquered: The Last Days of a Proud Queen

62. Dio Cassius, *Roman History*.

63. Dio Cassius, *Roman History*.

64. Dio Cassius, *Roman History*.

65. Dio Cassius, *Roman History*.

66. Plutarch, *Lives*.

67. Plutarch, *Lives*.

68. Plutarch, *Lives*.

69. Plutarch, *Lives*.

70. Plutarch, *Lives*.

71. Plutarch, *Lives*.

72. Dio Cassius, *Roman History*.

Chapter 8: A Woman for the Ages

73. Quoted in Hughes-Hallett, *Cleopatra*.

74. William Shakespeare, *Antony and Cleopatra*. Baltimore: Penguin Books, 1960.

75. Shaw, *Caesar and Cleopatra*.

76. Jon Solomon, *The Ancient World in the Cinema*. New York: A.S. Barnes and Company, 1978.

For Further Reading

Author's note: Some of these books deal with Cleopatra and her exploits, while others contain excellent descriptions of the important lands, peoples, beliefs, and events of her time.

Lionel Casson, *Daily Life in Ancient Egypt.* New York: American Heritage, 1975. Excellent presentation of ancient Egyptian customs, beliefs, royalty, professions, military, and so on. Contains many photos.

Alice Curtis Desmond, *Cleopatra's Children.* New York: Dodd, Mead and Company, 1971. This historical novel tells Cleopatra's story and also suggests what might have happened to her surviving children after her death. The author skillfully combines documented facts with imaginative but very believable supposition.

W.G. Hardy, *The Greek and Roman World.* Cambridge, MA: Schenkman Publishing, 1960. A good general overview of the Mediterranean classical world and how the political situations Cleopatra dealt with came to be.

Dorothy and Thomas Hoobler, *Cleopatra.* New York: Chelsea House, 1986. A competent, general synopsis of Cleopatra's life and legend.

Anthony Marks and Graham Tingay, *The Romans.* London: Usborne Publishing, 1990. A detailed, easy-to-read overview of Roman history, leaders, ideas, customs, beliefs, and institutions. Contains many colorful illustrations and handy maps.

Margaret A. Murray, *The Splendor That Was Egypt.* New York: Praeger Publishers, 1964. A fine general survey of ancient Egyptian civilization.

Richard Patrick, *Egyptian Mythology.* London: Octopus Books, 1972. A beautifully illustrated introduction to the gods and beliefs of the ancient Egyptians, which Cleopatra, for political reasons, publicly embraced.

Martha Rofheart, *The Alexandrian.* New York: Thomas Y. Crowell, 1976. A colorful historical novel about the legendary Egyptian queen, blending evidence from ancient writers like Plutarch and Appian with fictional situations and details.

Works Consulted

Appian, *Roman History*, translated by Horace White. Cambridge, MA: Harvard University Press, 1964. After two thousand years, Appian's epic history of Rome's civil wars is still riveting reading. Contains several important references to Cleopatra and much about Caesar, Antony, Octavian, and other key characters in her story.

Ernle Bradford, *Cleopatra*. New York: Harcourt, Brace, Jovanovich, 1972. Well-researched and impressively illustrated synopsis of Cleopatra's deeds and legend.

James Henry Breasted, *Ancient Times: A History of the Early World*. Boston: Ginn and Company, 1944. This classic study of the ancient world contains excellent discussions of Egyptian history, royalty, architecture, agriculture, and so on.

Julius Caesar, *War Commentaries of Caesar*, translated by Rex Warner. New York: New American Library, 1960. Caesar's fabulous exploits, including some of those in Egypt with Cleopatra, as told in his own words.

Cicero, *Letters to Atticus*, translated by E.O. Winstedt. Cambridge, MA: Harvard University Press, 1961. These fascinating letters of the Roman statesman Cicero cover three of his last four years, beginning in 46 B.C. He discusses the political situation in Rome, commenting on Caesar and his murderers. Cicero also expresses his personal dislike for Cleopatra.

Dio Cassius, *Roman History*, translated by Ian Scott-Kilvert. New York: Penguin Books, 1987. An excellent modern translation of Dio's important work about the events of Augustus Caesar's reign. Contains some of the most detailed passages about Cleopatra in ancient sources.

Michael Grant, *The World of Rome*. New York: New American Library, 1960. Excellent overview of ancient Roman culture.

Lucy Hughes-Hallett, *Cleopatra: Histories, Dreams and Distortions*. New York: HarperCollins Publishers, 1991. Extremely comprehensive study of Cleopatra, summarizing the known facts and also exploring later interpretations and spinoffs of her legend.

Flavius Josephus, *The Works of Flavius Josephus*, translated by William Whiston. Edinburgh, Scotland: William P. Nimmo, no date given. Collection of Josephus's works, including *The Antiquities of the Jews* and *The Wars of the Jews*. Josephus's commentaries on Cleopatra are among the few by non-Roman ancient historians that have survived.

Naphtali Lewis, *Life in Egypt Under Roman Rule*. Oxford, England: Clarendon Press, 1983. Good scholarly study of Roman influences on Egyptian culture.

Jack Lindsay, *Cleopatra*. London: Constable and Company, 1970. One of the best volumes about Cleopatra. Well researched and organized, it presents her deeds in the broader context of Mediterranean history in the first century B.C. Relies heavily on primary source quotes from ancient writers.

Pliny the Elder, *Natural History*, translated by H. Rackham. Cambridge, MA: Harvard University Press, 1967. Pliny's comprehensive study of the lands, peoples, plants, and animals of the Mediterranean world paints a vivid picture of the times. His description of one of Cleopatra's banquets has been endlessly quoted through the ages.

Plutarch, *Lives of the Noble Grecians and Romans*, translated by John Dryden. New York: Random House, 1932. Dryden's is one of the most widely used translations of Plutarch's writings. Extensive passages about Cleopatra are found in the *Life of Caesar* and the *Life of Antony*.

William Shakespeare, *Antony and Cleopatra*. Baltimore: Penguin Books, 1960. Shakespeare's magnificent stage play about the ill-fated romance of the title characters was based largely on Plutarch's *Lives*, especially the *Life of Antony*. Though it is seldom produced today, it is one of the author's greatest works. This edition is but one of dozens by different publishers, any of which will suffice.

George Bernard Shaw, *Caesar and Cleopatra*. Baltimore: Penguin Books, 1951. Shaw's stage version of the relationship between Caesar and the Egyptian queen is witty, funny, dramatic, literate, and immensely entertaining.

Jon Solomon, *The Ancient World in the Cinema*. New York: A.S. Barnes and Company, 1978. A fact-filled and critical study of the hundreds of movies based on ancient events and characters. Contains many references to and photos of the films about Cleopatra.

Suetonius, *Lives of the Twelve Caesars*, translated by J.C. Rolfe. Cambridge, MA: Harvard University Press, 1964. Although Suetonius, like most other Romans, tended to perpetuate Roman propaganda about Cleopatra, he also recorded important events in her life and those of her Roman lovers. An important ancient source.

Index

Picture Credits

Cover photo by Historical Pictures/Stock Montage

Alinari/Art Resource, NY, 7, 12, 20 (right), 45, 60, 66, 87, 93

The Bettmann Archive, 11 (bottom), 13 (bottom), 18, 20 (left), 21, 24, 26 (bottom), 27, 29, 33, 34, 35, 36, 39, 42, 44, 50, 52, 55, 58, 63, 64, 69, 72, 78, 89, 91, 94, 95, 97

Brown Brothers, 59, 70

Culver Pictures, Inc., 8, 23, 32, 43, 54, 75, 76, 79, 80, 82, 84, 96, 99

Foto Marburg/Art Resource, NY, 31

Giraudon/Art Resource, NY, 57, 68

North Wind Picture Archives, 9, 11 (top), 13 (top), 14, 15, 17, 26 (top), 38, 40, 48, 51, 61, 73, 92

Sipa Press/Art Resource, NY, 19

About the Author

Don Nardo is an actor, film director, and composer, as well as an award-winning writer. His writing credits include more than forty books, including *Gravity, Animation, Anxiety and Phobias, The Mexican-American War,* and biographies of Thomas Jefferson, Joseph Smith, H.G. Wells, Charles Darwin, and Jim Thorpe. Among his other writings are short stories, articles, teleplays and screenplays for ABC Television, and feature films. Thematically, *Cleopatra* is a companion piece to Lucent's other books *Ancient Greece, The Roman Republic,* and *The Roman Empire,* Mr. Nardo's trilogy of classical civilization. He lives with his wife Christine on Cape Cod, Massachusetts.